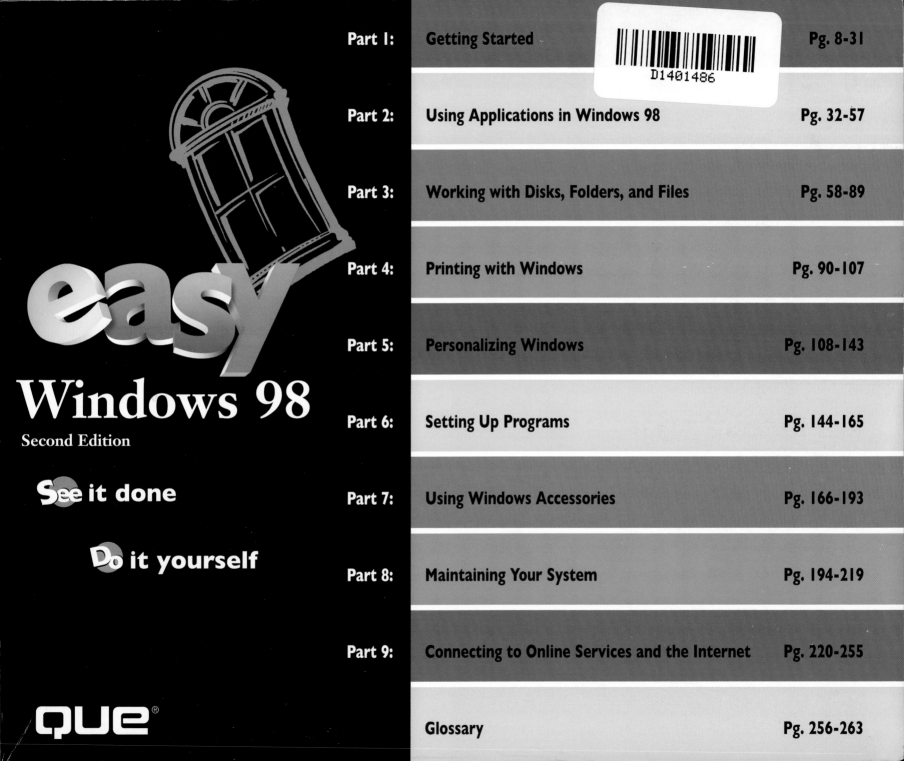

easy
Windows 98
Second Edition

See it done

Do it yourself

que®

D1401486

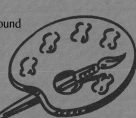
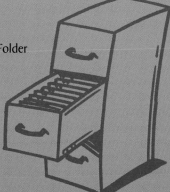

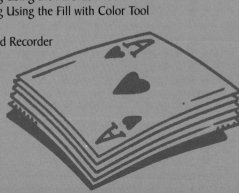

Copyright© 1999 by Que® Publishing

International Standard Book Number: 0-7897-2245-3

Library of Congress Catalog Card Number: 98-85097

01   00   4   3

Interpretation of the printing code: The rightmost double-digit number is the year of the book's printing; the rightmost single-digit, the number of the book's printing. For example, a printing code of 99-1 shows that the first printing of the book occurred in 1999.

Composed in Baker Signet by Macmillan Computer Publishing

Printed in the United States of America

Publisher:	Greg Wiegand
Executive Editor:	Chris Will
Director of Editorial Services:	Lisa Wilson
Managing Editor:	Thomas F. Hayes

About the Author

Shelley O'Hara works as a freelance writer in Indianapolis. She is the author of over 60 books, including several best-selling titles. O'Hara was the author of the first set of Easy books. She graduated with a BA in English from the University of South Carolina and also has an MA in English from the University of Maryland.

Dedication

To Sean Michael O'Hara

Acknowledgments

The credit for this book should be shared among the team that helped edit, design, and lay out the pages, especially my wondrous editor, Kate Welsh, and the book's production designers, Stacey DeRome, Ayanna Lacey, and Heather Miller. I am indebted to all for their remarkable work and to everyone else who was a part of this series.

Development Editor
Kate Shoup Welsh

Project Editor
Linda Seifert

Indexer
Chris Barrick

Technical Reviewer
John Purdum

Editorial Coordinator
Mandie Rowell

Editorial Assistant
Lori Morgan

Cover Designers
Anne Jones
Karen Ruggles

Book Designer
Jean Bisesi

Copy Writer
Eric Borgert

Production Designers
Stacey DeRome
Ayanna Lacey
Heather Miller

Proofreader
Maribeth Echard

How to Use this Book

It's as Easy as 1-2-3

Each part of this book is made up of a series of short, instructional lessons, designed to help you understand basic information that you need to get the most out of your computer hardware and software.

 Click: Click the left mouse button once.

 Double-click: Click the left mouse button twice in rapid succession.

 Right-click: Click the right mouse button once.

 Pointer Arrow: Highlights an item on the screen you need to point to or focus on in the step or task.

 Selection: Highlights the area onscreen discussed in the step or task.

 Click & Type: Click once where indicated and begin typing to enter your text or data.

 Tips and Warnings give you a heads-up for any extra information you may need while working through the task.

2 Each task includes a series of quick, easy steps designed to guide you through the procedure.

How to Drag: Point to the starting place or object. Hold down the mouse button (right or left per instructions), move the mouse to the new location, then release the button.

1 Each step is fully illustrated to show you how it looks onscreen.

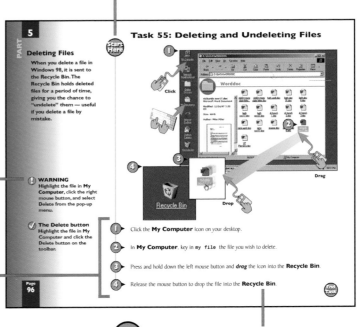

3 Menus, dialog boxes, tabs, windows, and items you click are shown in **Bold**.

Next Step: If you see this symbol, it means the task you're working on continues on the next page.

 End Task: Task is complete.

Introduction to Easy Windows 98

Becoming proficient with a new operating system—such as Windows 98—can seem like a daunting task. There's so much to learn: How do you create and edit documents? How can you customize the desktop? How do you connect to the Internet? Sometimes these questions can seem overwhelming.

That's why *Easy Windows 98* provides concise, visual, step-by-step instructions for handling all the tasks you'll need to accomplish. You'll learn how to get started in Windows 98, how to use applications, how to organize your materials, how to print, how to personalize your system, how to set up programs, how to use Windows accessories, how to maintain your system, how to connect to online services, and more.

You can choose to read the book cover to cover, or to use it as a reference when you encounter a piece of Windows 98 that you don't know how to use. Either way, *Easy Windows 98* lets you see it done and do it yourself.

Getting Started

Windows 98 is the newest version of Windows. Introduced in 1998, this version includes some new features designed to make your computer easier to use. If you purchased a new computer recently, this is the version you most likely have. You can also upgrade to Windows 98 by purchasing the new version from a retail store or from Microsoft.

You don't need to do anything to start Windows 98 other than turn on your PC. When you turn on your computer, Windows starts automatically, and you see a screen called the *desktop*. The desktop is your starting point. Here you find the key tools for working with your computer. From your Windows desktop, you can open and switch between applications, search for specific folders, print documents, and perform other tasks. This section covers the basics of working with the desktop.

Tasks

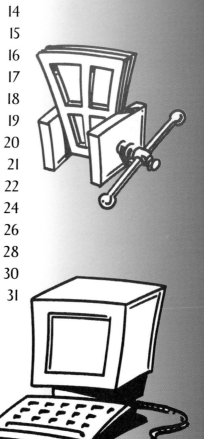

Task 1: Displaying the Start Menu

The taskbar, located at the bottom of your screen, contains the **Start** button. Clicking the **Start** button enables you to start applications, open documents you recently had open, customize settings in Windows, get help, and more. You use the **Start** button to begin most tasks in Windows.

Click

Click

✓ Close Menu

If you click the **Start** button by mistake and want to close the **Start** menu without choosing a command, simply click outside the menu.

1 ▶ Click the **Start** button.

2 ▶ Click the command you want.

Task 2: Opening a Window

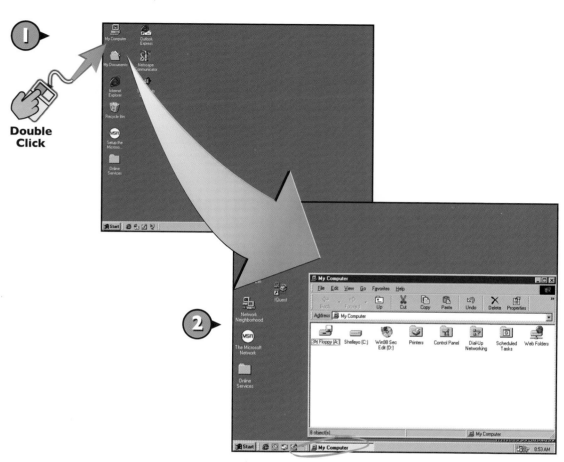

Double Click

Windows 98 displays all its information in onscreen boxes called *windows*. To work with any of the information on your computer, you must know how to display (or open) these windows. Most windows are represented onscreen by small pictures called *icons*. You can double-click an icon to display the contents of the window the icon represents.

① Double-click the **My Computer** icon.

② The contents of this icon are displayed, and a button for the **My Computer** window appears on the taskbar.

✓ **Nothing Happens?**
If nothing happens when you double-click an icon, it might be because you did not click quickly enough or because you single-clicked, moved the mouse, and single-clicked again. You have to click twice in rapid succession. A good way to practice using the mouse is to play solitaire.

✓ **Single-Click**
If your desktop is set up as a Web desktop (covered later in this book), you can simply single-click to open an icon.

Task 3: Closing a Window

You close a window after you finish working with it and its contents. Too many open windows clutter the desktop as well as the taskbar.

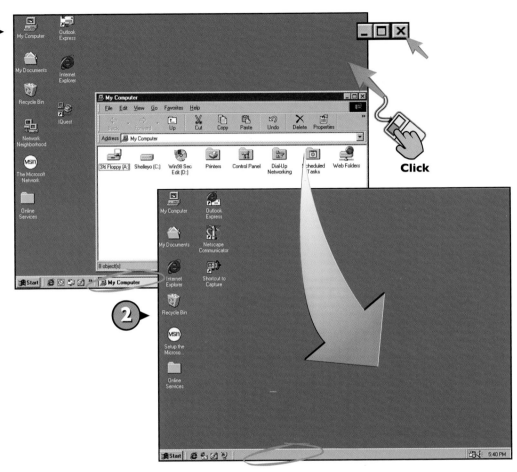

Click

✓ **Use the Control Menu**
The **Control** menu, located in the upper-left corner of the title bar, contains commands related to the open window, such as **Restore, Move, Size, Close,** and so on. To close the window via the **Control** menu, click the **Control Menu** icon and then choose **Close** from the menu. Alternatively, you can press **Alt+F4**.

① Click the **Close** button (the button marked with an × in the top-right corner of the **My Computer** window).

② The window is closed, and the button for the window no longer appears in the taskbar.

End Task

Task 4: Minimizing a Window

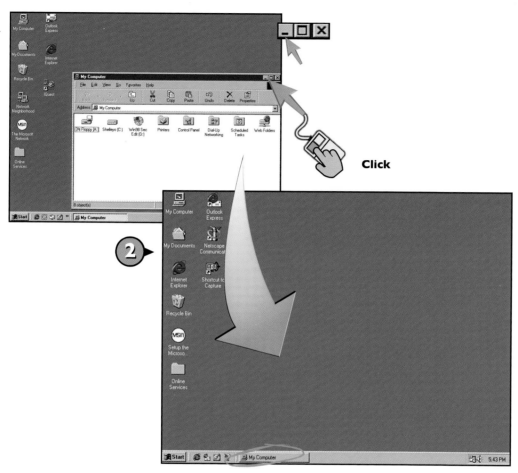

Click

You can reduce (minimize) a window so that it is still available as a taskbar button, but is not displayed on the desktop. You might want to minimize a window to temporarily move it out of your way, but keep it active for later use.

 Click the **Minimize** button in the window you want to minimize.

 The window disappears from the desktop, but a button for this window remains on the taskbar.

 Check Taskbar
You can tell which windows you have open by looking at the taskbar.

Task 5: Maximizing a Window

You can enlarge (maximize) a window so that it fills the entire screen. Doing so gives you as much room as possible to work in that window.

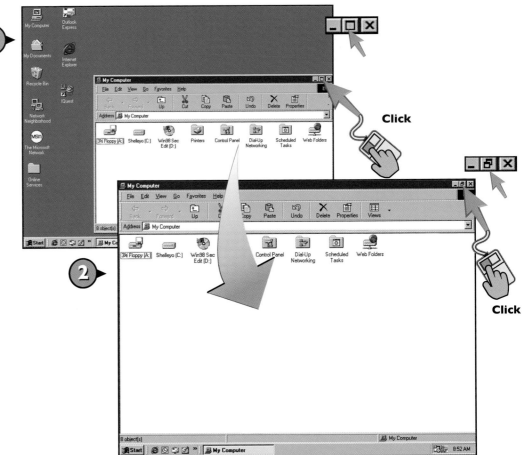

Click

Click

 Click the **Maximize** button.

 The window enlarges to fill the screen, and the **Maximize** button changes to the **Restore** button.

Task 6: Restoring a Window

Start Here

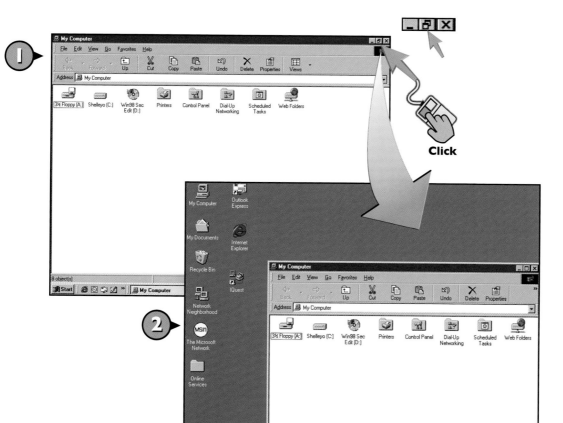

Click

If you maximize a window, you can easily restore it to its original size.

 In a maximized window, click the **Restore** button.

 The window is restored to its original size.

End Task

As you add more applications, folders, shortcuts, and so on to the desktop, you'll need more room to display these elements. You can easily move the windows around so you can see all the open windows at one time.

Task 7: Moving a Window

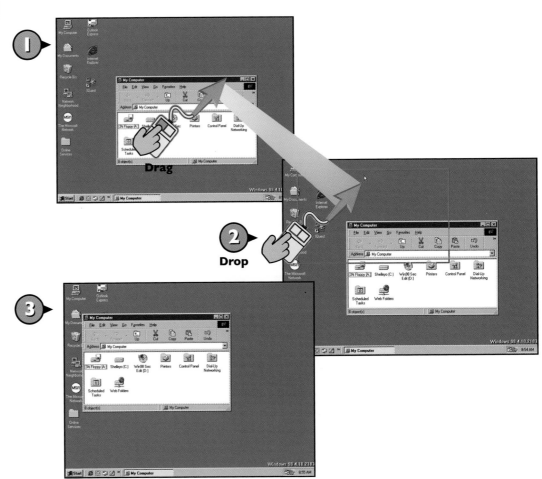

Start Here

Drag

Drop

✓ **Title Bar**
Be sure to point to the title bar. If you point to any other area, you might resize the window instead of moving it.

1 To move an open window, point to its title bar. Click and hold down on the mouse button.

2 Drag the window to a new position. You can see the border of the window as you drag. Release the mouse button.

3 The window and its contents appear in the new location.

End Task

Task 8: Resizing a Window

Start Here

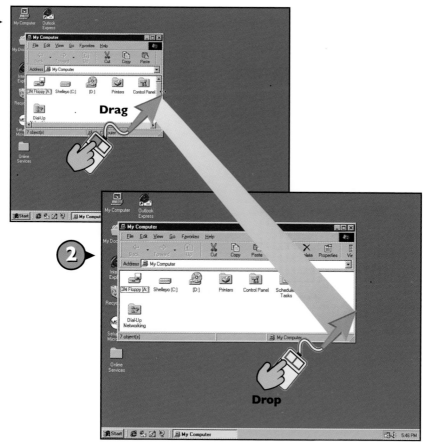

In addition to being able to move a window, you can resize a window to whatever size you want. Resizing windows is helpful if you want to view more than one window at the same time.

✓ Resize from Corner
You can drag a corner of the window to proportionally resize both dimensions (height and width) at the same time.

✓ No Borders?
You cannot resize a window that is maximized. If you don't see borders, you cannot resize the window. If you want to resize the window, simply restore it and then resize it.

1 ► Point to any window border. You should see a double-headed arrow.

2 ► Drag the border to resize the window, and then release the mouse button. The window is now resized.

Task 9: Scrolling a Window

If a window is too small to show all its contents, horizontal and vertical *scrollbars* appear along the edges of the window. You can use these bars to scroll through the window to see the other contents.

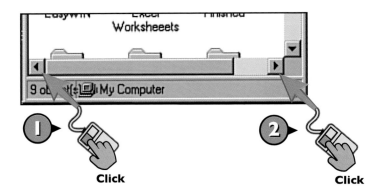

Click   Click

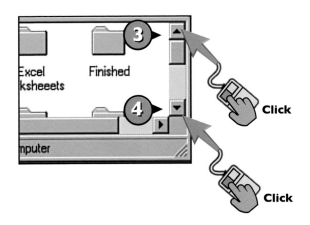

Click

Click

✓ **Click for Fast Scrolling**
You can click anywhere in the scrollbar to jump in that direction to another part of the window. You can also click the scroll box to scroll quickly through the window.

1 ▶ Click the left arrow to scroll left through the window.

2 ▶ Click the right arrow to scroll right through the window.

3 ▶ Click the up arrow to scroll up through the window.

4 ▶ Click the down arrow to scroll down through the window.

Task 10: Using Menus

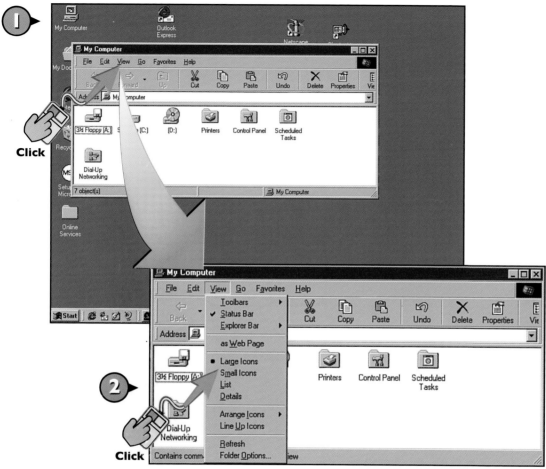

Click

Click

Although you can perform many tasks by clicking the mouse on different onscreen objects, you must choose commands to perform the majority of Windows tasks. Commands are organized in menus to make them easy to find. Most windows contain menu bars that list the available menus; each menu then contains a group of related commands.

1 In the window or program, click the menu name (in this case, the menu name is **View**).

2 Click the command you want.

✓ **See an Arrow?**
Selecting a command that is followed by an arrow will display a submenu. Clicking a command that is followed by an ellipsis will display a dialog box.

✓ **Close Menu**
To close a menu without making a selection, press the **Esc** button on your keyboard or click outside the menu.

End Task

Task 11: Using Shortcut Menus

Shortcut menus, also called *quick menus* and *pop-up menus*, provide common commands related to the selected item. You can, for example, quickly copy and paste, create a new folder, move a file, or rearrange icons using a shortcut menu.

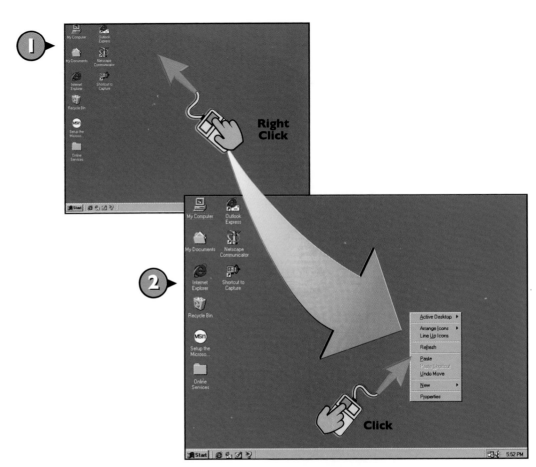

Right Click

Click

Menus Vary
Different shortcut menus appear depending on what you're pointing to when you right-click the mouse.

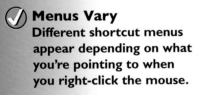 Right-click the item for which you want to display a shortcut menu. For instance, right-click any blank part of the desktop.

Click the command you want in the shortcut menu.

Page 20

End Task

Task 12: Arranging Windows on the Desktop

Start Here

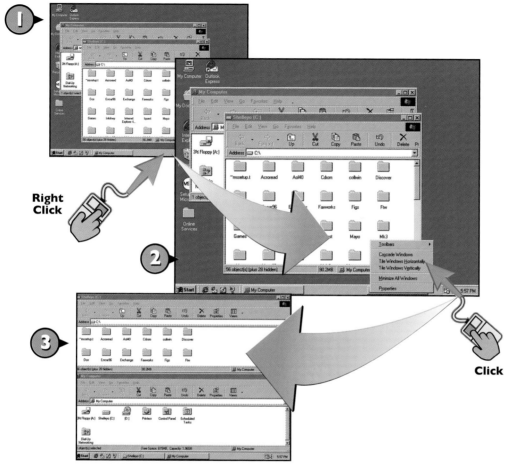

Right Click

Click

As you work, you will often have several windows open on the desktop at one time. The windows probably overlap each other, which can make it difficult to find what you want. To make your work easier and more efficient, Windows enables you to arrange the windows on the desktop in several different ways.

✅ **Select Window**
To work in any one of the open windows, click the desired window to make it active. The active window moves to the front of the stack, and its title bar is a different color.

✅ **Right-Click Blank Part**
Be sure to right-click on a blank area, not on a button.

✅ **Undo**
Undo the arrangement by right-clicking again and choosing **Undo**.

1️⃣ With multiple windows on the desktop, right-click a blank area of the taskbar.

2️⃣ Click the arrangement you want.

3️⃣ Windows arranges the windows; here they are tiled horizontally.

End Task

Task 13: Using a Dialog Box

When you choose certain commands, a dialog box prompts you for additional information about how to carry out the command. Dialog boxes are used throughout Windows; luckily, all dialog boxes have common elements and all are treated in a similar way.

✓ Dialog Boxes Vary

Different dialog boxes will have different options. The figures in this section are meant to show the types of items you might find in a dialog box.

✓ Radio Buttons and Check Boxes

Dialog boxes contain various types of elements, including radio buttons and check boxes. You can choose only one radio button within a group of radio buttons; choosing a second option deselects the first. However, you can select multiple check boxes within a group of check boxes.

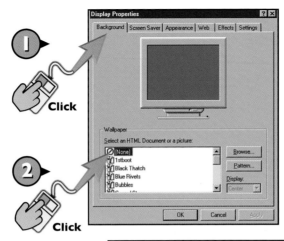

Click

Click

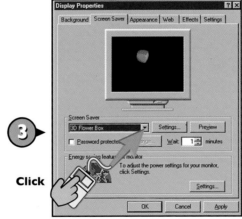

Click

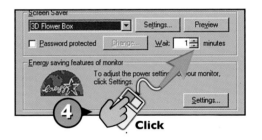

Click

1. To view a tab, click it.

2. To use a list box, scroll through the list and click the item you want to select.

3. To use a drop-down list box, click the arrow and then select the desired item from the list.

4. To use a spin box, click the arrows to increment or decrement the value or type a value in the text box.

Next Step

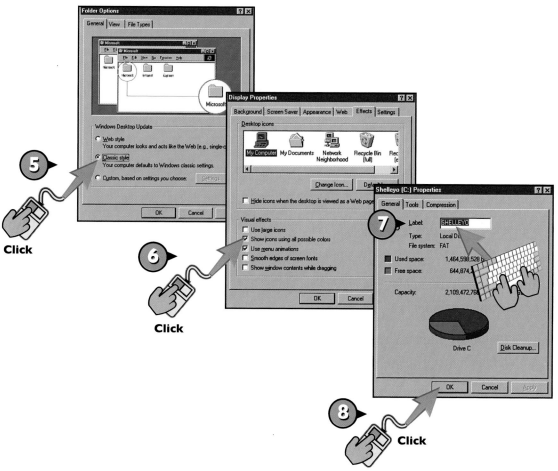

Click

Click

5 ▶ Click a radio button to activate it.

6 ▶ Click a check box to select it (or to deselect a check box that is already checked).

7 ▶ Type an entry in a text box.

8 ▶ After you make your selections, click the **OK** button.

✓ **Make a Selection**
When a dialog box is open, you cannot perform any other action until you accept any changes by clicking the **OK** button. To close the dialog box without making a selection, click the **Cancel** button.

End Task

Task 14: Looking Up a Help Topic in the Table of Contents

Use the **Contents** tab to locate help for performing specific procedures, such as printing a document or installing new software. The specific topics included in the **Contents** tab quickly refer you to everyday tasks you might need to perform in the program.

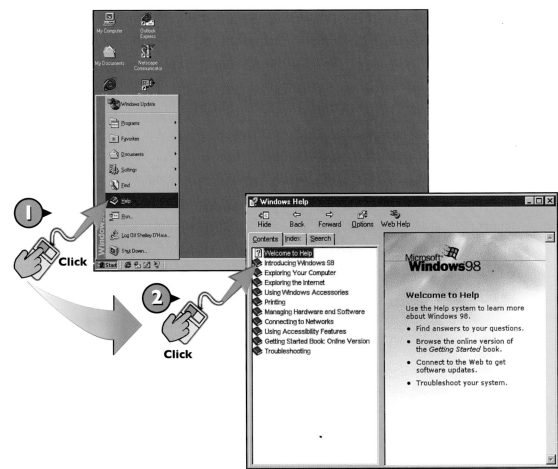

✓ **Print Type**
Click the **Options** button and then choose **Print** to print the help topic.

✓ **Definitions**
You can click any of the underlined text in the help area to display a definition of that term or to display related help information.

1 Click the **Start** button, then select **Help**.

2 Click the topic you want help on.

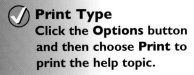

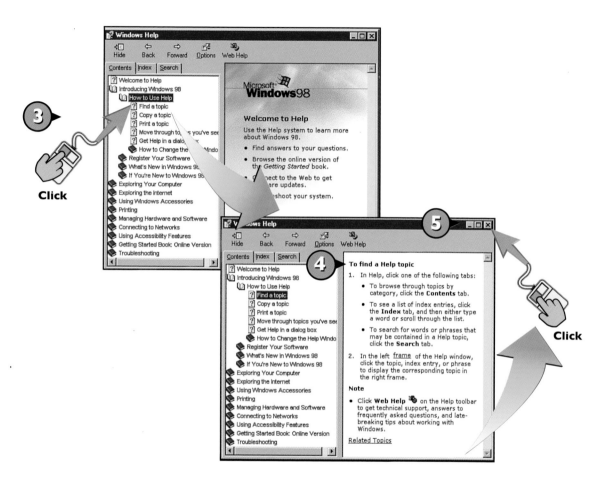

Click

Click

③ Continue clicking book topics until you find the exact help topic you need, then click that help topic.

④ Review the help information.

⑤ Click the **Close** button to close the **Help** window.

✓ **Look for Book**
Subtopics are indicated with a book icon.

✓ **Look for Question Mark**
Help topics are indicated with a question mark icon.

Task 15: Looking Up a Help Topic in the Index

If you want to find help on a specific topic, such as storing files by size or editing text, use the **Index** tab in the **Help** window. Topics listed in the index are in alphabetical order. You can quickly scroll to see topics of interest.

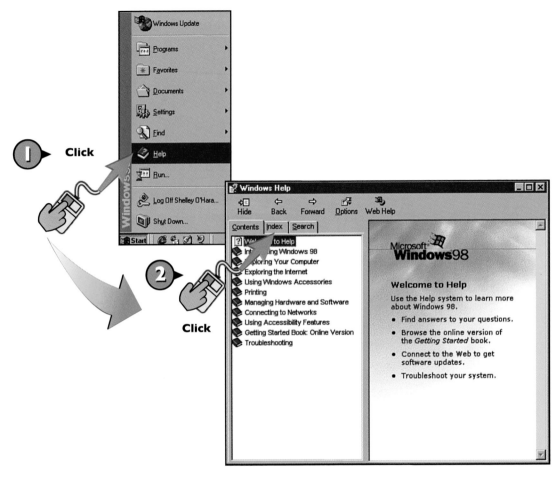

Click

Click

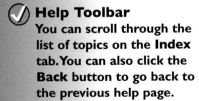

Help Toolbar
You can scroll through the list of topics on the **Index** tab. You can also click the **Back** button to go back to the previous help page.

 Click the **Start** button, then select **Help**.

 Click the **Index** tab in the **Windows Help** dialog box.

Next Step

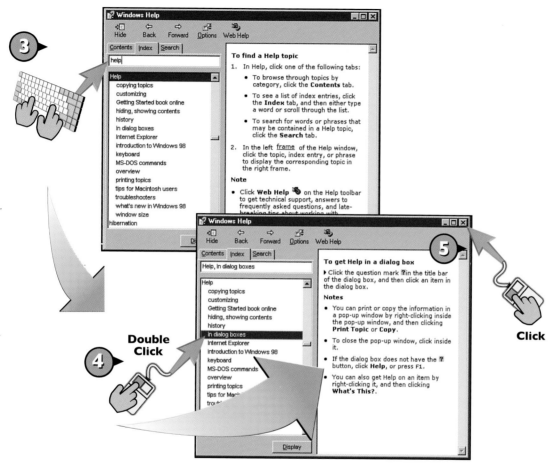

Double Click

Click

3 ▶ Type the topic for which you want to find help. The list below the text field jumps to the topic you type.

4 ▶ Double-click the topic you want to review and look over the help information.

5 ▶ Click the **Close** button.

Task 16: Searching for a Help Topic

If you don't find the topic in the table of contents or index, try searching for it. Windows will display a list of topics that contain what you are looking for; you can then select the one you want.

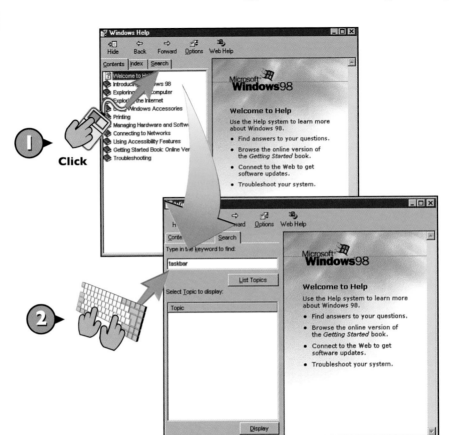

Click

✓ **Help Works the Same**
Windows help works in the same way throughout most Windows applications. If you master help basics, you can apply these same skills to other programs.

 Click the **Search** tab in the **Windows Help** dialog box (to get to this dialog, refer to Task 15).

 Type the topic you want to find.

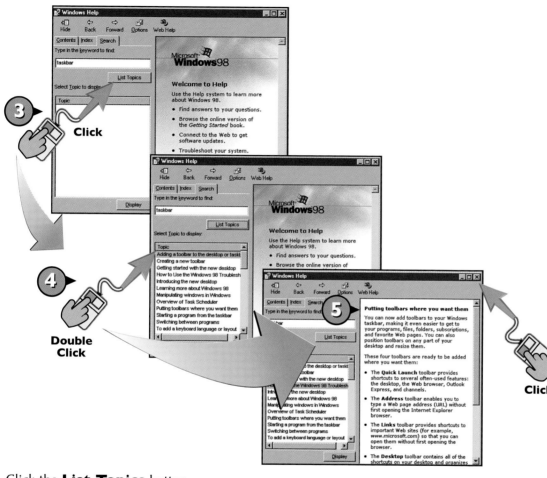

Click

Double Click

Click

 Get Online Help

If you are connected to the Internet, you can use **Web Help** to get product support from Microsoft's Web site. Click the **Web Help** button and then log on to your Internet provider. Use any of the links to get help. For more information on the Internet, see Part 9, "Connecting to Online Services and the Internet."

3 ▶ Click the **List Topics** button.

4 ▶ Double-click the topic you want to review.

5 ▶ Review the help information, then click the **Close** button.

End Task

Task 17: Getting Context-Sensitive Help

When you open a dialog box, you might not know what each of the options does. If you have a question about an option, you can view a description of that option by following the steps in this task.

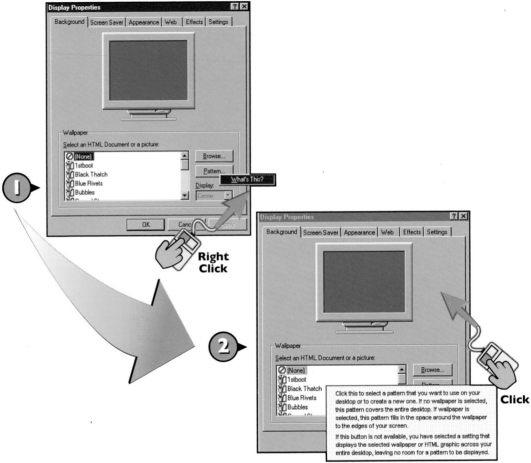

Right Click

Click

 In a dialog box, right-click the option you want help on, then click the **What's This?** command.

 After you review the material in the pop-up explanation, click anywhere within the dialog box to close the pop-up box.

Task 18: Shutting Down the Computer

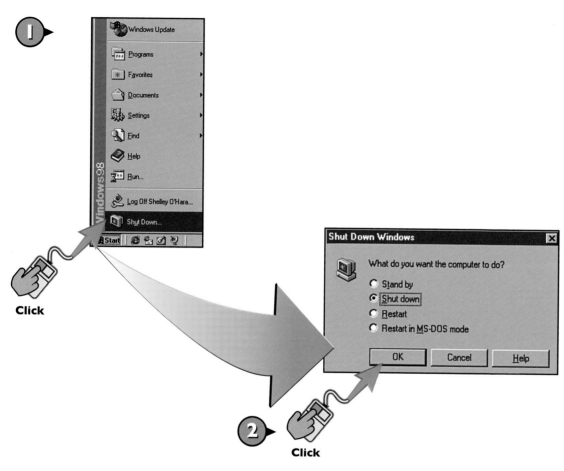

Click

Click

If you turn off the power to your computer before you properly shut the computer down, you could lose valuable data or damage an open file. Windows provides a safe shutdown feature that checks for open programs and files, warns you to save unsaved files, and prepares the program for you to turn off your computer. You should always shut down before you turn off the power.

 Other Options
Sometimes you might need to work from DOS instead of Windows. To boot to DOS, choose the **Restart in MS-DOS** mode option in the **Shut Down Windows** dialog box, and then choose **OK**. You can also choose **Restart** to restart the computer.

1. After you've closed down all open programs, click **Start** and then **Shut Down**.

2. Select the **Shut down** radio button and click **OK**.

 Cancel Shutdown
If you don't want to shut down Windows, choose **Cancel**.

PART 2

Using Applications in Windows 98

One advantage of using Windows 98 is the enormous number of available Windows applications. You can use many word-processing, database, spreadsheet, drawing, and other programs in Windows. This variety of applications provides you with all the tools you need to perform your everyday tasks.

Windows applications are easy to open and use, and enable you to save data in files of different names and in various locations on your hard disk or a floppy disk. You can open a file at any time to view, edit, or print it. This part covers starting and working with applications.

Tasks

Task 1: Starting an Application from the Start Menu

Most of the time you spend using your computer will be with an application. You can start an application in any number of ways, including from the **Start** menu. When you install a new Windows application, that program's installation procedure will set up a program folder and program icon on the **Start** menu.

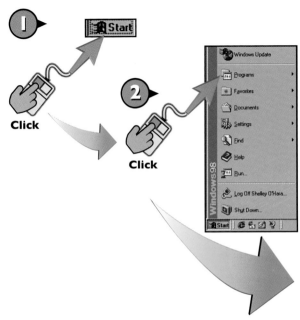

Click

Click

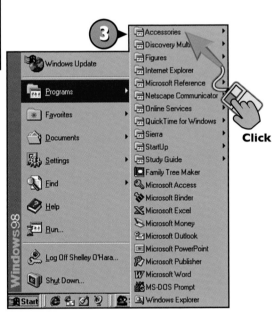

Click

 Click the **Start** button.

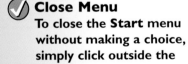

✔ **Close Menu**
To close the **Start** menu without making a choice, simply click outside the menu.

 Click the **Programs** command.

Click the program group that contains the application you want to start (in this case, **Accessories**).

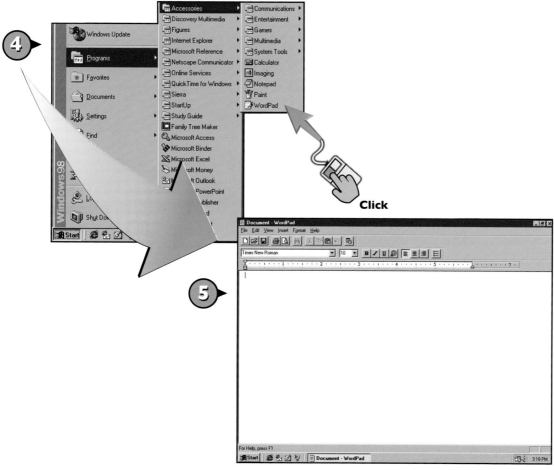

Click

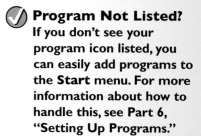

4 ▶ Click the application you want to start.

5 ▶ The application opens in its own window.

 Program Not Listed?
If you don't see your program icon listed, you can easily add programs to the **Start** menu. For more information about how to handle this, see Part 6, "Setting Up Programs."

Task 2: Starting an Application from a Shortcut Icon

If you frequently use a certain program, you might want to be able to access that program right from the desktop. To do so, you can set up a shortcut icon (covered in Part 6) and then start the program by double-clicking that icon.

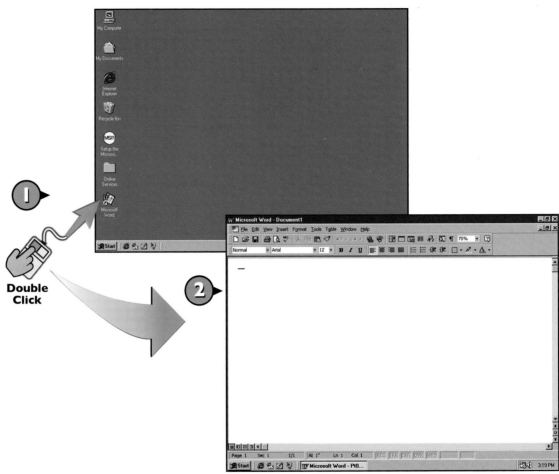

Double Click

✓ Nothing Happens?
If nothing happens when you double-click the icon, or if the icon moves, it might be because you haven't clicked quickly enough or because you clicked and dragged by accident. Be sure to press the mouse button twice quickly.

 Double-click the shortcut icon on the desktop.

2 The application is started and displayed in its own window.

Task 3: Starting an Application and Opening a Document

Start Here

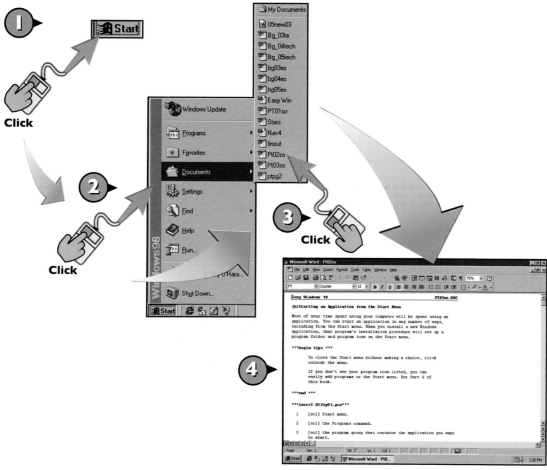

Click

Click

Click

Click

If you want to work on a document that you recently had open (in Word, for example), you can use a shortcut to both start Word and open the document. Windows 98's **Documents** menu lists the 15 documents that you have opened most recently.

① Click the **Start** button.

② Click **Documents**.

③ Click the document you want to work on (in this case, **Pt02so**).

④ The program for that document is started and the document is opened.

✓ **Clear Documents Menu**
To clear the **Documents** menu, click the **Start** menu, choose **Settings**, and then choose **Taskbar & Start Menu**. Click the **Start Menu Programs** tab and click the **Clear** button.

End Task

Task 4: Switching Between Applications

Because you most likely work with more than one type of document, you need a way to switch from one program to another. For example, you might want to compare price figures from an Excel worksheet with a price list you've set up in Word. Switching between applications enables you not only to compare data, but also to share data.

Start Here

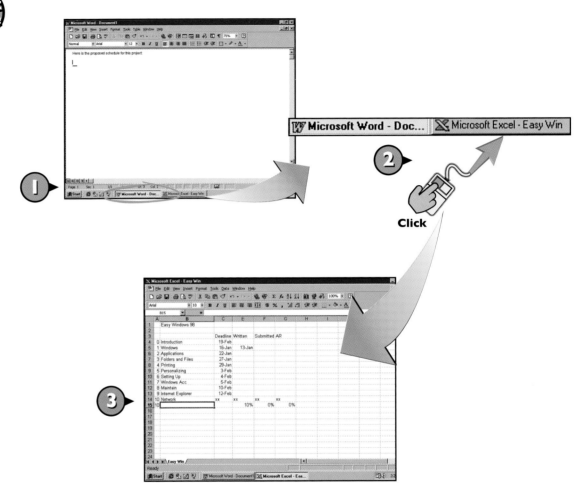

Click

✓ How Many?
The number of programs you can have open at any one time depends on the amount of RAM (random-access memory) in your system.

✓ What's Running?
You can tell what programs are open by looking at the taskbar. Each open program is represented by a button; the button representing the program you are currently using is selected.

1 After you've started two programs, look at the taskbar. You should see a button for each program. In this case, the **Microsoft Word** button is selected; Microsoft Word is displayed onscreen.

2 Click the button for the program you want to switch to (in this case, Microsoft Excel).

3 Excel becomes the active program.

End Task

Task 5: Closing an Application

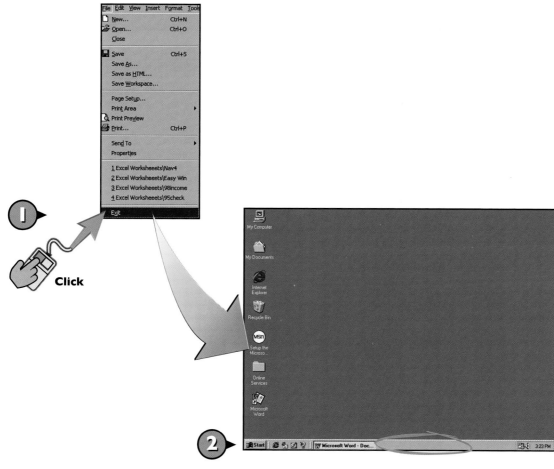

Click

When you finish working in an application, close it to free system memory. Too many open applications can tax your system's memory and slow the computer's processes, such as saving, printing, switching between applications, and so on.

✓ **More Ways**
To close an application, you can also press **Alt+F4** or click the **Close** button in the application's title bar.

✓ **Save First!**
If you have not saved a file and choose to close that file's application, a message box appears asking if you want to save the file. If you do, click **Yes**; if not, click **No**. If you want to return to the document, click **Cancel**. For more information, see the next task.

1 Click **File** and then click the **Exit** command.

2 The program is closed. Notice that the taskbar button for Excel has disappeared.

End Task

Task 6: Saving a Document

You save documents and files so that you can refer to them later for printing, editing, copying, and so on. The first time you save a file, you must assign that file a name and folder (or location). You save documents pretty much the same way in all Windows applications; this task shows you how to save a document in Word.

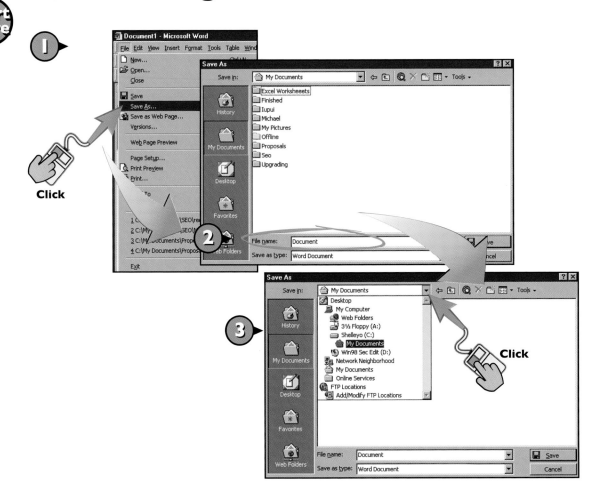

Click

Click

✅ **Save Again**
After you've saved and named a file, you can simply click **File** and select **Save** to resave that file to the same location with the same name. Any changes you have made since the last save are reflected in the file.

✅ **Save with New Name**
To save the file with a different name or in a different location, use the **Save As** command and enter a different filename or folder.

1 ▸ Click **File**, and then click the **Save As** command.

2 ▸ The program might propose a name for the file. You can either accept this name or type a new name.

3 ▸ To save the document in another drive, click the **Save in** drop-down list and select the drive you want.

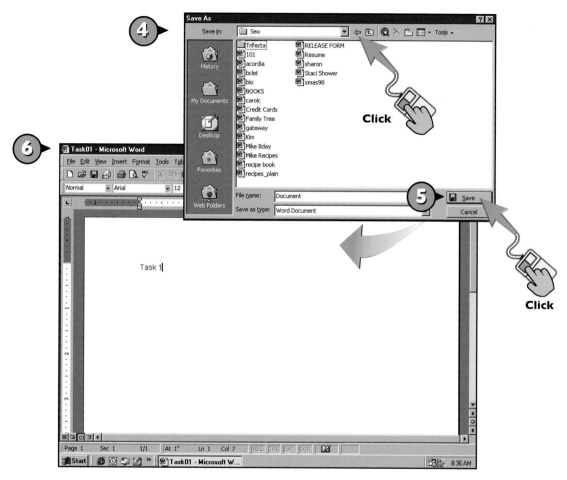

4 ► To save the document in another folder, click the desired folder in the list. To move up through the folder structure, click the **Up One Level** button.

5 ► Click the **Save** button.

6 ► The application saves the file and returns to the document window. The document name is listed in the title bar.

✓ **New Tools**
Office 2000 programs include a revamped **Save As** dialog box with new features for selecting a folder.

✓ **Illegal Characters**
You cannot use any of the following characters in a filename:

: " ? * < > / \ |

You can, however, use spaces, letters, and numbers.

Task 7: Opening a Document

The purpose of saving a
document is to make it
available for later use. You
can open any of the
documents you have saved
by selecting **File** and
choosing the **Open**
command.

Click

Double Click

Click

✅ **Can't Find a File?**
If you can't find the file you
want to work with, it could
be because you did not
save it where you thought
you did. Try looking in a
different drive or folder. If
you still can't find it, try
searching for the file (for
more information about
searching for files, see Part
3, "Working with Disks,
Folders, and Files").

1 ▶ Click **File**, and then click the **Open** command.

2 ▶ If the file you need is listed in the dialog box, double-click it and skip the remaining steps.

3 ▶ If the file is not listed, display the **Look in** drop-down list and select the drive where you
placed the file.

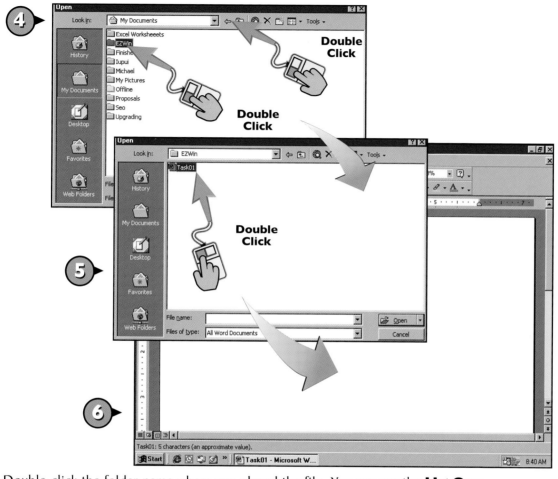

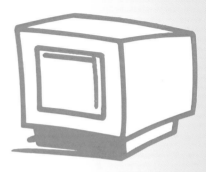

④ ▶ Double-click the folder name where you placed the file. You can use the **Up One Level** button to move up through the folder structures.

⑤ ▶ When you find the file you seek, double-click it.

⑥ ▶ The file is opened.

Shortcut
As a shortcut, click **File.** You'll notice that the last files opened are listed near the bottom of the menu. You can open any of these files by clicking them in the **File** menu.

Task 8: Switching Between Open Documents

You can work with several documents in your application, opening as many documents as the program allows. Simply click **File** and select the **Open** command to open the files you want to work with. Then you can easily switch between any of the open documents.

✓ **Switching Documents Versus Applications**
Don't confuse switching between documents with switching between applications. For more information, refer to Task 4, "Switching Between Applications."

✓ **Arrange Windows**
You can arrange all open documents in the window to make your desktop easier to manage. Click **Window**, select the **Arrange All** command, and then choose the arrangement you want.

✓ **Active Window**
The active document's title bar will be a different color from the other documents' title bars.

Click

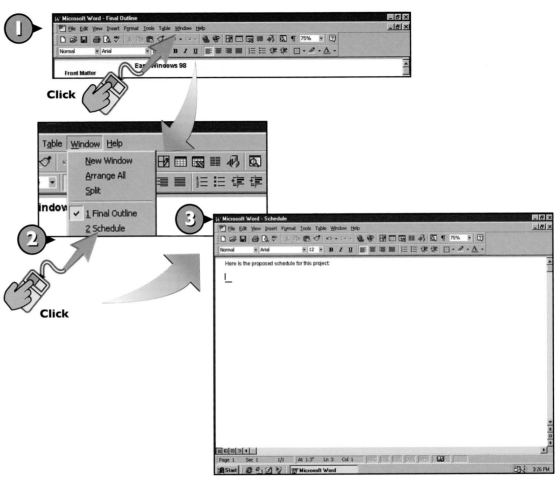

Click

Click

1 ▶ Click **Window**.

2 ▶ Notice that the current document has a check mark next to its name. Click the document that you want to switch to (in this case, the document called **Schedule**).

3 ▶ The document you just clicked in the **Window** menu becomes the active document.

Task 9: Creating a New Document

Start Here

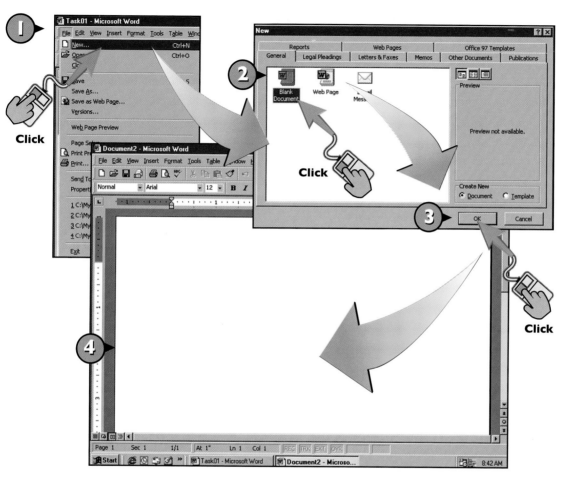

When you want a new "sheet" of paper, you can create a new document. For complex programs like PowerPoint (a presentation program) and Access (a database program), you might be prompted to make some selections before the new document is created. For others, you simply select the template you want. (A *template* is a predesigned document.)

 Click **File**, and then click the **New** command.

 If you see a **New** dialog box, click the type of document you want to create.

 Click the **OK** button.

 A new document is displayed.

Shortcut
As a shortcut, you can click the **New** button to create a new document based on the default template.

End Task

Task 10: Closing a Document

When you save a document, it remains open so that you can continue working. If you want to close the document, you can easily do so. You should close documents that you are no longer using in order to free up memory.

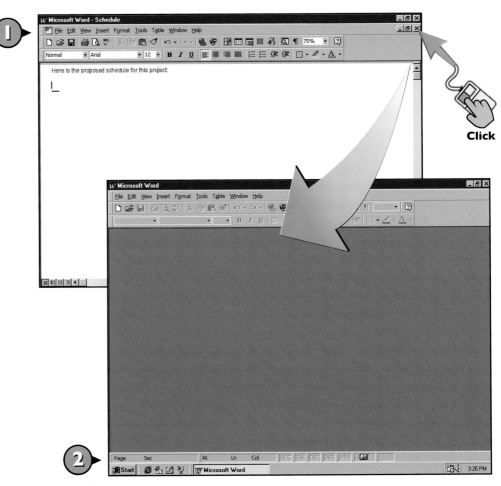

Click

✓ **Exit Program**

If you click the **Close** button on the program window, you exit the program. Be sure to use the **Close** button for the document window if you want to remain in the program but close the document.

✓ **Doxument Window Controls**

In most programs, the document window has its own set of controls—separate from the controls for the program window. You can move, resize, maximize, minimize, and close the document window using the skills you learned in Part 1.

 Click the **Close** button.

The document is closed, but the program remains open. You can create a new document or open an existing document.

Task 11: Selecting Text

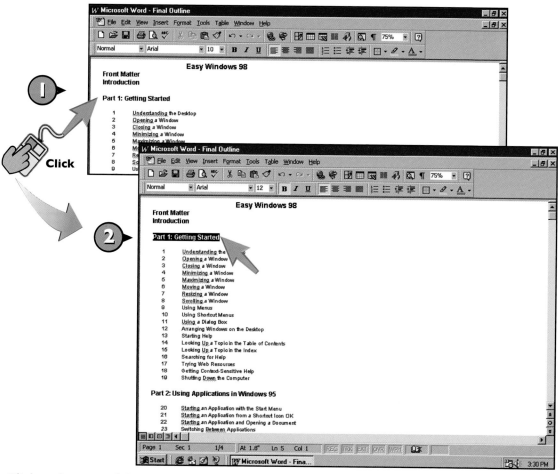

One of the primary skills you need for working with data is knowing how to select what you want to work on. For instance, you can select text and then delete it, move it, copy it, change its appearance, and more.

Click

1. Click at the start of the text you want to select.

2. Hold down the mouse button and drag across the text, then release the mouse button. The selected text appears highlighted.

✓ **Use Keyboard**
If you prefer to use the keyboard to select text, hold down the **Shift** key and use the arrow keys to highlight the text you want to select.

✓ **Deselect Text**
To deselect text, click outside the text.

End Task

Task 12: Copying Text

One of the most common editing tasks is to copy text. You can copy text and paste the copy in the current document or in another document.

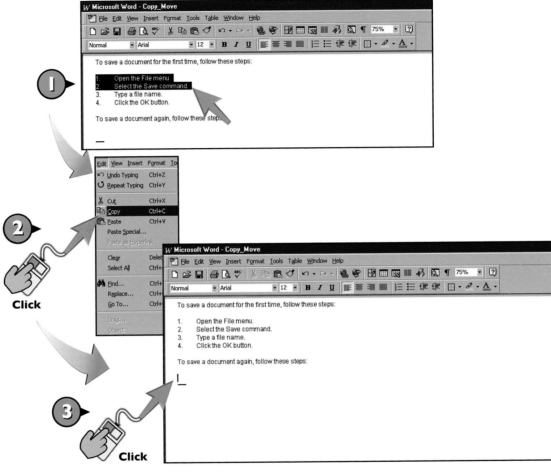

✓ Copy to Another Document
To copy data from one open document to another, select the text and then move to the document where you want to paste the text using the **Window** menu.

1 ▶ Select the text you want to copy.

2 ▶ Click **Edit**, and then select the **Copy** command.

3 ▶ Click the spot in the document where you want to put the copied data.

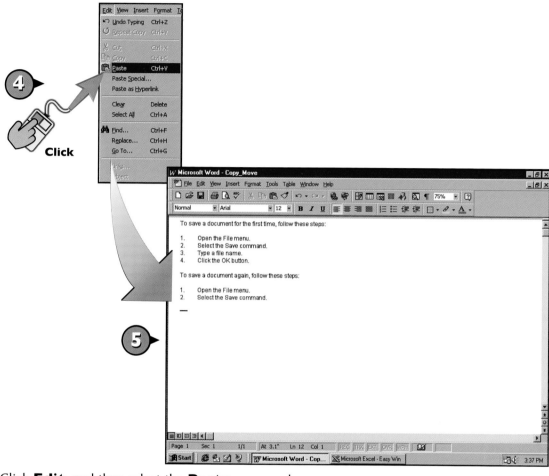

Edit View Insert Format T
- ↶ Undo Typing   Ctrl+Z
- ↺ Repeat Copy   Ctrl+Y
- ✂ Cut   Ctrl+X
- 📋 Copy   Ctrl+C
- 📋 **Paste**   Ctrl+V
- Paste Special...
- Paste as Hyperlink
- Clear   Delete
- Select All   Ctrl+A
- 🔍 Find...   Ctrl+F
- Replace...   Ctrl+H
- Go To...   Ctrl+G
- Links...
- Object...

Click

4 ▶ Click **Edit**, and then select the **Paste** command.

5 ▶ The data is pasted into the document.

✓ **Copy to Another Application**
For information about copying data from one application to another, see Task 14, "Copying Data Between Applications."

End Task

Task 13: Moving Text

Just as you can copy text, you can move text from one location in a document to another location in the same document. You can also move text from one document to another. Moving text is similar to copying text, except that when you move something it is deleted from its original location.

✔ **Move to Another Application**
For help on moving data from one application to another, see Task 15, "Moving Data Between Applications."

✔ **Undo Move**
You can undo a paste operation if you change your mind after performing the action. Simply click **Edit** and then select the **Undo Paste** command to remove the text you just pasted.

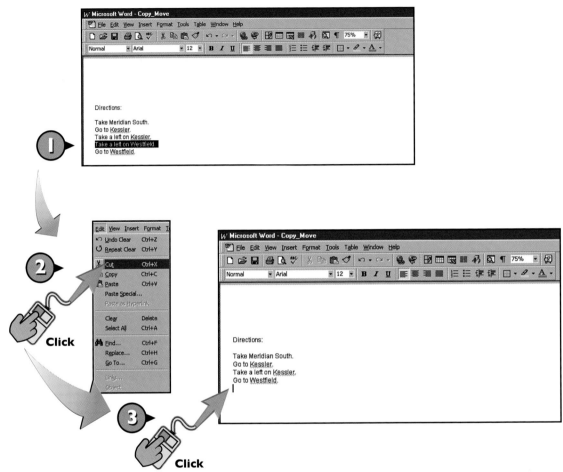

Click

Click

1 Select the text you want to move.

2 Click **Edit**, and then click the **Cut** command. Windows deletes the data from the document and places it in the **Clipboard**, a temporary holding spot.

3 Click in the document where you want to place the text.

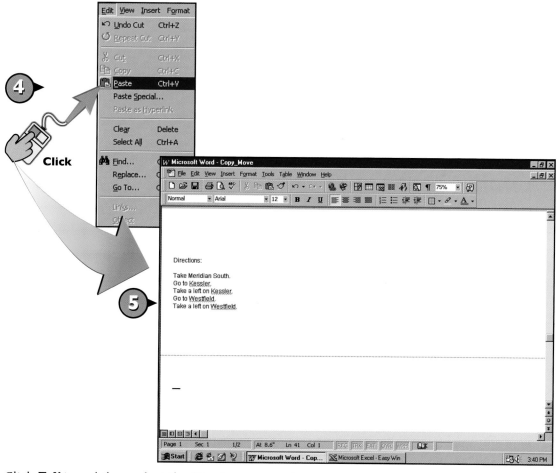

4 Click **Edit**, and then select the **Paste** command.

5 The text is pasted into the new location.

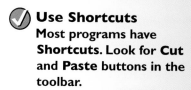

✓ **Use Shortcuts**
Most programs have **Shortcuts**. Look for **Cut** and **Paste** buttons in the toolbar.

Task 14: Copying Data Between Applications

You can copy data from a document in one application and paste it into another document in another application to save time typing. In addition to being able to copy text, you can copy spreadsheets, figures, charts, clip art, and so on. Using copied text and graphics saves you time in your work.

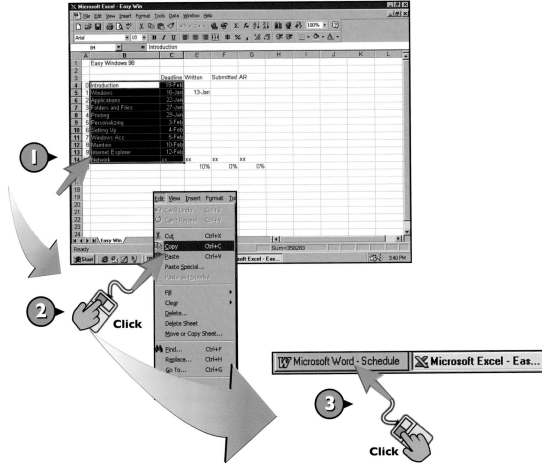

Start Here

Click

Click

✓ **Keyboard Shortcuts**
You can also use the keyboard shortcut **Ctrl+C** to copy and the keyboard shortcut **Ctrl+V** to paste. Also look for toolbar buttons for **Copy** and **Paste**.

1 ▶ Select the data you want to copy.

2 ▶ Click **Edit**, and then click the **Copy** command.

3 ▶ Click the taskbar button representing the program you want to switch to (in this case, Microsoft Word). If the program isn't started, start the program.

Next Step

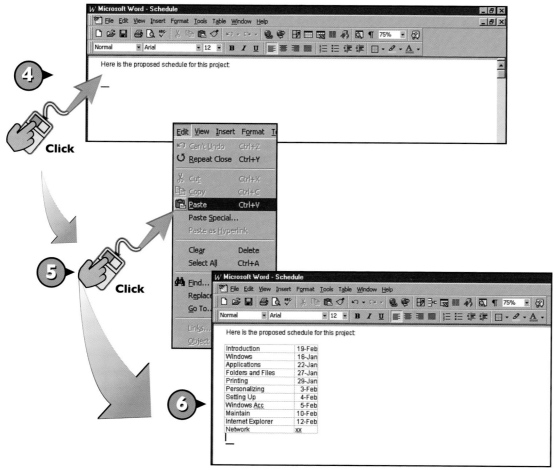

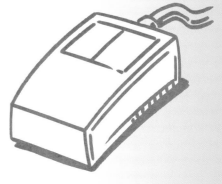

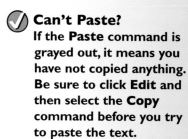

④ In the Word document, click the location where you want to paste the copied data.

⑤ Click **Edit**, and then click the **Paste** command.

⑥ The data is pasted into the document.

✓ **Can't Paste?**
If the **Paste** command is grayed out, it means you have not copied anything. Be sure to click **Edit** and then select the **Copy** command before you try to paste the text.

Task 15: Moving Data Between Applications

You can also move information from one application to another. For instance, you can cut a table of numerical data from Excel and paste into a report in Word.

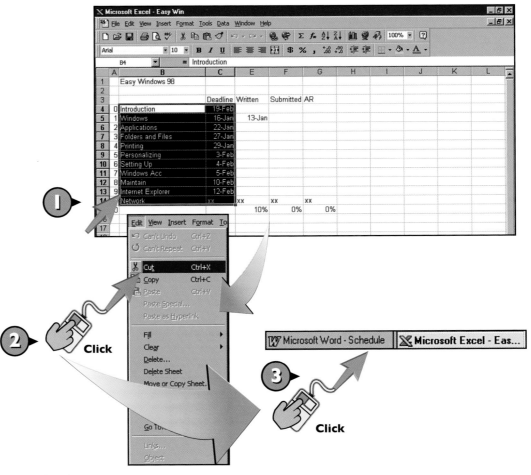

Shortcuts
You can also use the keyboard shortcut **Ctrl+X** to cut, and use the keyboard command **Ctrl+V** to paste. Look also for toolbar buttons for **Cut, Copy,** and **Paste.**

 Select the data you want to move.

 Click **Edit**, and then click the **Cut** command. Windows deletes the data from the document and places it in the **Clipboard**, a temporary holding spot.

 Click the taskbar button representing the program you want to switch to (in this case, Microsoft Word).

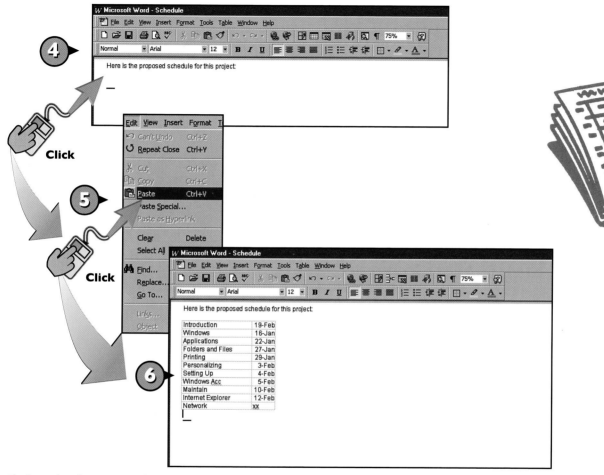

④ Click in the document where you want to place the data.

⑤ Click **Edit**, and then click the **Paste** command.

⑥ The data is pasted into the document.

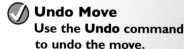

Undo Move
Use the **Undo** command to undo the move.

Task 16: Linking Data Between Applications

You might link data between applications if you want the data to be updated automatically when you edit or add to the source document. Linking data saves you time because you only have to edit the information once; Windows then updates any linked files for you.

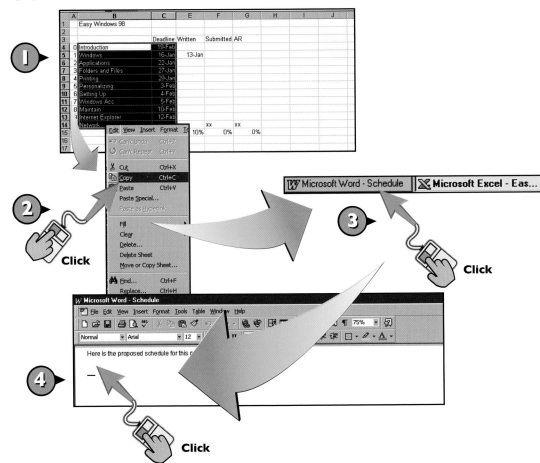

✓ **Update Links**
Check the program documentation for commands on updating and maintaining links.

1 In the source document, select the data you want to link.

2 Click **Edit**, and then click the **Copy** command.

3 Click the taskbar button representing the program and document where you want to paste the linked data.

4 Click in the document where you want the linked data to go.

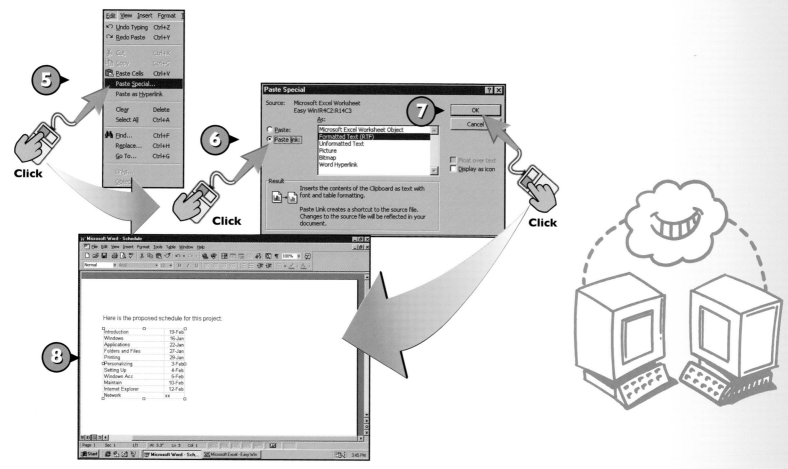

5 Click **Edit**, and then click the **Paste Special** command.

6 Select the **Paste Link** radio button, and then select the format you want to paste from the **As** list box.

7 Click the **OK** button.

8 Windows inserts the data with a link between the destination and the source files.

✓ **Formats**
The available formats in the As list box depend on the type of data you're pasting and control how the data is inserted into the document.

End Task

PART

Working with Disks, Folders, and Files

One part of working with Windows is learning how to work with the documents you save and store on your system. Think of your computer's hard drive as a filing cabinet. To keep your files organized, you can set up folders. Folders on the hard drive represent drawers in the filing cabinet, and each folder can hold files or other folders. (In previous versions of Windows, folders were called directories.) You can open and close folders, view a folder's contents, copy and move folders, and create or delete folders.

The more you work on your computer, the more files and folders you add. After a while, your computer will become cluttered, and you'll need a way to keep these files organized. Windows provides features that can help you find, organize, and manage your files. You can copy files, move files, delete unnecessary files, and more. For working with files and folders, you can use either **My Computer** or **Windows Explorer**, as covered in this section.

Tasks

Task 1: Opening Folders

Folders contain files, programs, or other items that you can use to do work in Windows. You can display the contents of a folder to work with the files—move a file, create a shortcut icon, start a program, and so on.

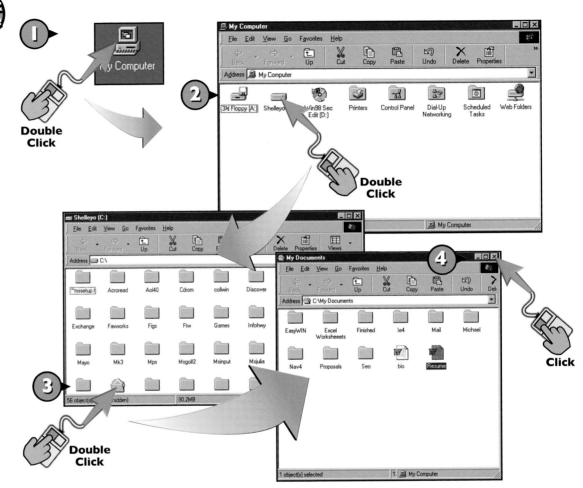

✓ Scroll Through the Window
Remember that you can use the scrollbars to scroll through the window. Also, you can move and resize the window as needed.

✓ Change the View
You can select how the contents of a folder are displayed. See Tasks 4, "Changing How the Contents of a Window Are Displayed," and 6, "Changing the View Style" later in this part.

✓ Close Window
To close a window and all its associated windows, hold down the **Shift** key and click the **Close** button.

1 ▶ Double-click the **My Computer** icon on the desktop.

2 ▶ Double-click the icon representing your hard drive (usually **C**:).

3 ▶ Each icon that you see represents a folder on your hard drive. Double-click any of the folders.

4 ▶ Each file folder icon represents groups of files and folders. Each page icon represents a document. Click the **Close** button to close the window.

End Task

Task 2: Editing a Document Using Toolbar Buttons

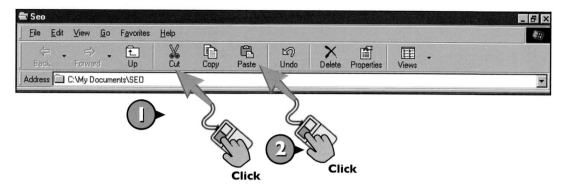

Click **Click**

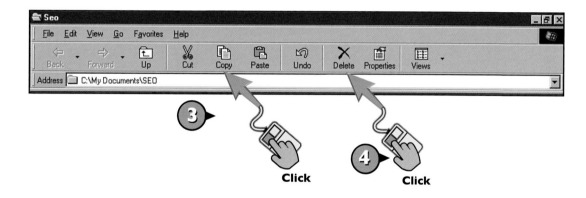

Click **Click**

The buttons in the toolbar have shortcuts for moving and copying files and folders. You can also delete files and folders.

1 Click the **Cut** button to cut the selected item (file or folder).

2 Click the **Paste** button to paste the item you cut or copied.

3 Click the **Copy** button to copy the selected item.

4 Click the **Delete** button to delete the selected item.

Button Name
If you aren't sure what a toolbar button does, put the pointer on the button. A ToolTip name pops up.

Task 3: Using the Toolbar Buttons in a File Window

Each window, whether it's a file or folder window, includes a toolbar that you can use to quickly change drives or directories in the window and to change views of the folder contents.

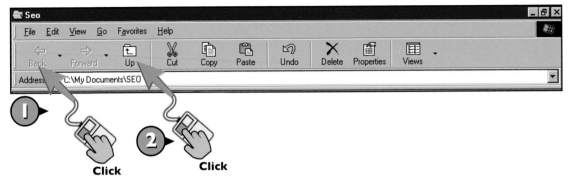

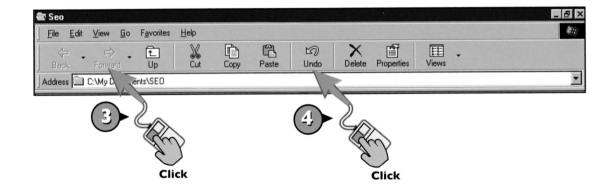

Click the **Back** button to go back to a previously viewed page.

Click the **Up** button to display the next level up in the folder structure.

Click the **Forward** button to go forward (after going back) to a previously viewed page.

Click the **Undo** button to undo the last action.

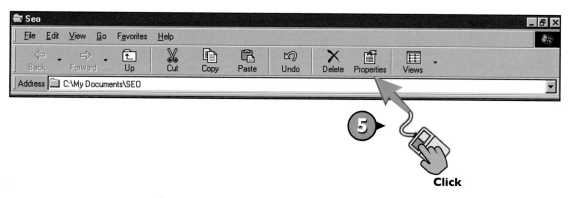

5 ▶ Click the **Properties** button to display the **Properties** dialog box with additional information about the selected item.

6 ▶ Click the **Address** button to select another folder or drive from the drop-down list.

7 ▶ Click the **Views** button to select a different view.

 Similar to Web Browsing
The toolbar buttons are similar to those in a Web browser.

Task 4: Changing How the Contents of a Window Are Displayed

You can view the contents of a window in a variety of ways. By default, Windows uses large icons to display the contents of a window. If you want to see more of a window's contents at one time, you can change the view to **Small Icons**. You can also display such details about an item as its type, its size, and the date it was last modified. Changing the way a window displays its contents can make it easier to find what you need.

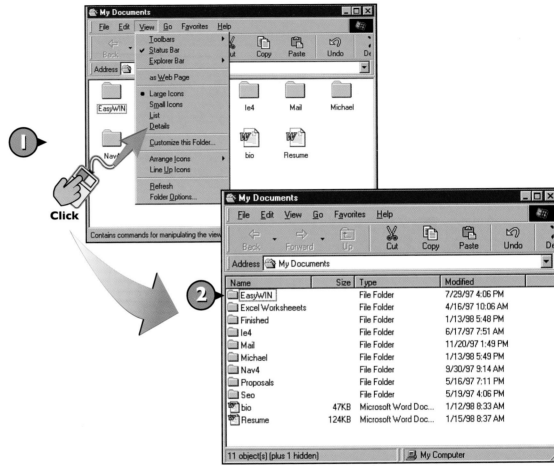

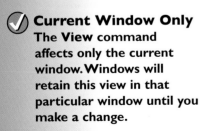

Current Window Only
The **View** command affects only the current window. Windows will retain this view in that particular window until you make a change.

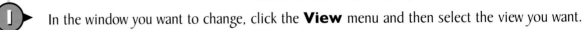

1. In the window you want to change, click the **View** menu and then select the view you want.

2. The window displays the contents in that view (in this case, the **Details** view).

End Task

Task 5: Sorting the Contents of a Window

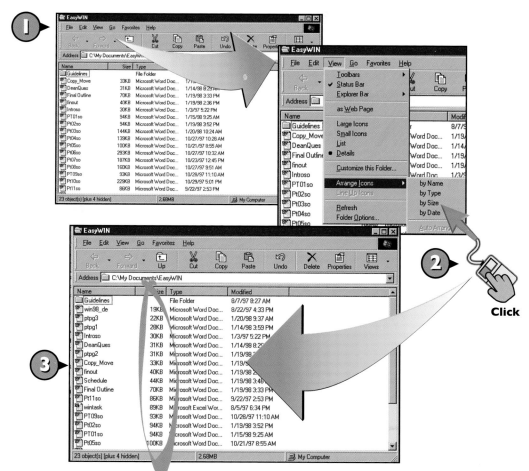

Click

You sort the contents of a window so that you can more easily find the files you want. Windows enables you to arrange the files in a folder by name, type, date, and size. Sorting the files is even easier if you choose to view them by the file details first. You can sort files viewed as large or small icons or as a list.

✓ **Sort Orders**
You can also sort by name in alphabetical order, by file type, or by date from oldest to most recent by choosing the appropriate command from the **Arrange Icons** submenu. You can also click the column header in **Details** view to sort by that column.

✓ **My Computer Sorts**
If you are working in the **My Computer** window, you have different options for arranging the icons. You can arrange by type, size, drive letter, or free space.

1 ▶ Open the window you want to sort and change to the view you want. In this case, the window is displayed in **Detail** view so that you can see the results of sorting by different columns.

2 ▶ Click **View**, select the **Arrange Icons** command, and choose the sort order you want (in this case, **by Size**).

3 ▶ Windows sorts the files in the selected order. For instance, this view shows the files sorted by size from the smallest to largest.

End Task

Task 6: Changing the View Style

You can choose to display the contents of a window as *links*, which makes working with that window similar to browsing the Internet or an *intranet* (an internal network set up like the Internet). With a single click, you can open files, folders, or drives.

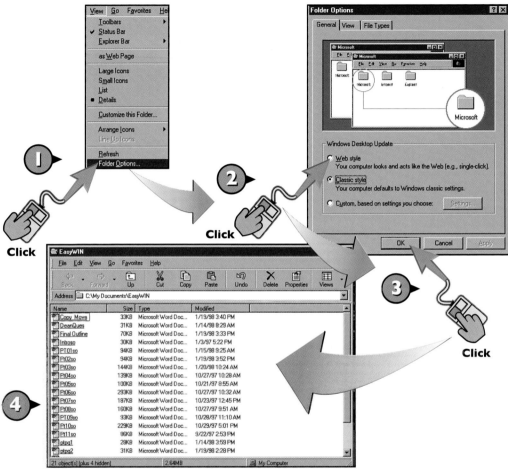

Click

Click

Click

Click

✓ **Back to Classic**
To return to the Classic style, open the **View** menu and choose the **Folder Options** command. Choose **Classic style** and click the **OK** button.

✓ **More Internet Information**
For more information on the Internet, see Part 9, "Connecting to Online Services and the Internet."

① Click **View**, and then select the **Folder Options** command.

② Click the **Web style** radio button.

③ Click the **OK** button.

④ The contents of the window are displayed in **Web** view, so working with the window is similar to browsing a Web page. The folders and files are displayed as links.

Task 7: Working in Web View

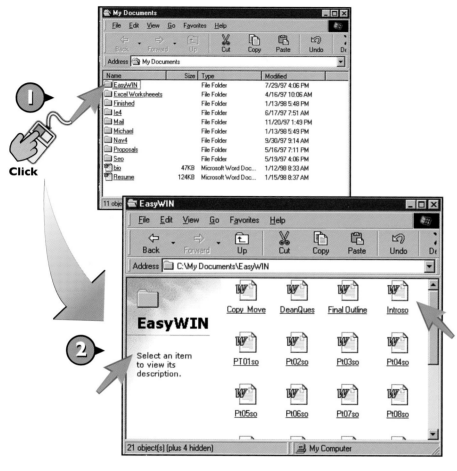

Click

In **Web** view, you can single-click an item to activate it. You can also view more information about the window contents in two separate panes.

✓ **Back to Classic**
To go back to the **Classic** style, open the **View** menu and choose the **Folder Options** command. Choose **Classic style** and click the **OK** button.

✓ **Menu Command**
The **Web Page** command under the **View** menu is turned on automatically.

✓ **Customize Web View**
You can customize the view to your own settings. Click the **View** menu, select the **Folder Options** command, and choose **Custom**. Click the **Settings** button, and then make your selections. After you're satisfied with the selections you've made, click the **OK** button.

1 After you've selected **Web** view (see the preceding task), the contents of the window should look similar to a Web page. Click any of the folders once.

2 The left pane displays information about the selected item. The right pane displays the contents of the selected folder.

Task 8: Creating a Folder

Working with your files is easier if you group related files into folders. For example, you might want to create a folder in your word-processing program's folder to hold all the documents you create with that program. Creating a folder enables you to keep your documents separated from the program's files so you can easily find your document files.

Start Here

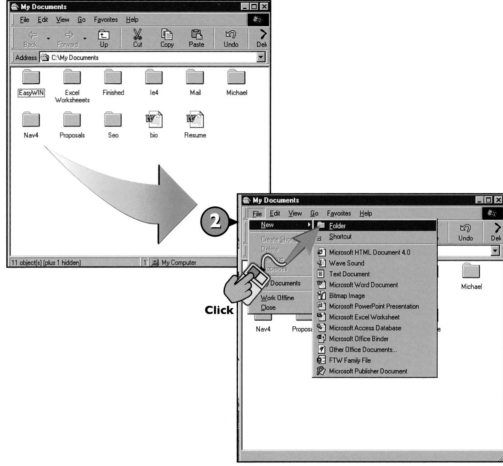

Click

✓ Delete a Folder
If you change your mind about the new folder, you can always delete it. To delete the folder, select it and then press the **Delete** key on your keyboard. Click the **Yes** button to confirm the deletion.

1 Open the window for the folder or disk where you want to create the new folder.

2 Click **File**, select the **New** command, and then click **Folder**.

Next Step

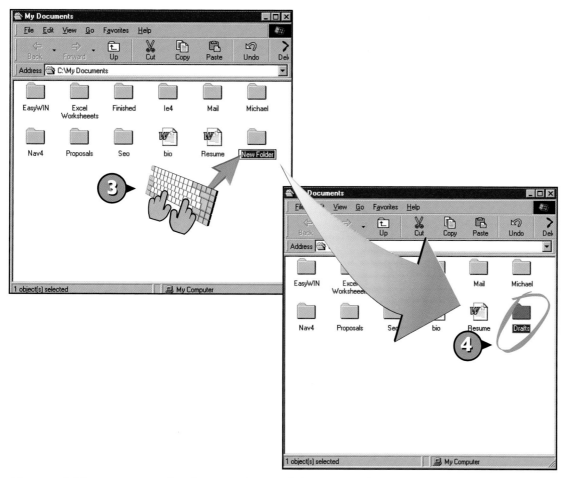

 The new folder appears in the drive window, and the name is highlighted. To change the name of the folder, type a new name and press **Enter**.

 The folder is added.

✅ **Create New Documents**
You can also use the **New** command to create shortcuts or certain document types.

✅ **Folder Name**
The folder name can contain as many as 255 characters, and can include spaces.

Task 9: Copying Folders

Windows 98 makes it easy for you to copy a folder and its contents and then paste them in a new location. You can, for example, copy a folder to a floppy disk to use as a backup or to move to another computer. In addition, you can copy a folder and its contents to another location on the hard drive if, for example, you want to revise the original file for a different use.

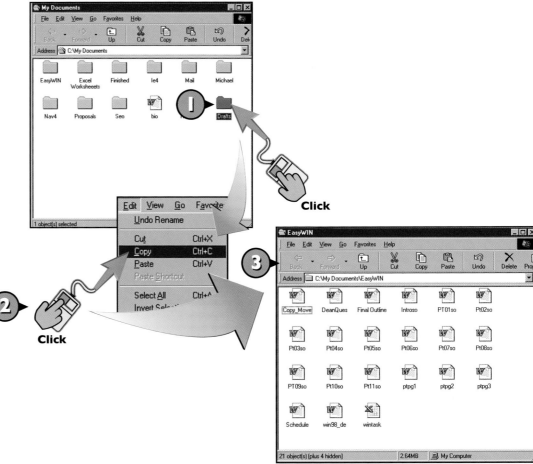

✅ Drag a Copy

You can copy a folder by first opening both the window that contains the folder (the source) and the window to which you want to copy the folder (the destination). Click the folder in the source window and drag it to the destination window.

✅ Use Buttons

You can also use the **Copy** button or right-click the folder and choose **Copy** from the shortcut menu.

① ▶ Select the folder you want to copy.

② ▶ Click **Edit**, and then select the **Copy** command.

③ ▶ Open the folder or drive where you want to paste the copy.

Next Step

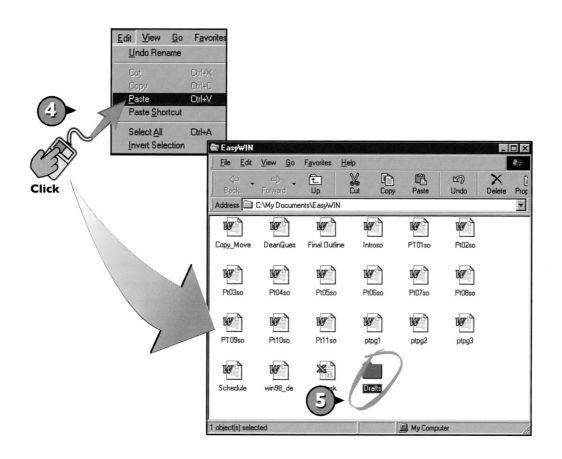

 Click **Edit**, and then select the **Paste** command.

 Windows copies the new folder and its contents to this location.

 What's Copied?
Keep in mind that you copy both the folder and its contents. If you don't need the copy, you can delete it. See Task 12, "Deleting Folders," for more information.

Task 10: Moving Folders

You can move a folder and its contents to another folder or to a disk so that you can reorganize your directory structure. For example, you might want to move all related files and folders to the same place on your hard drive so you can find them quickly and easily.

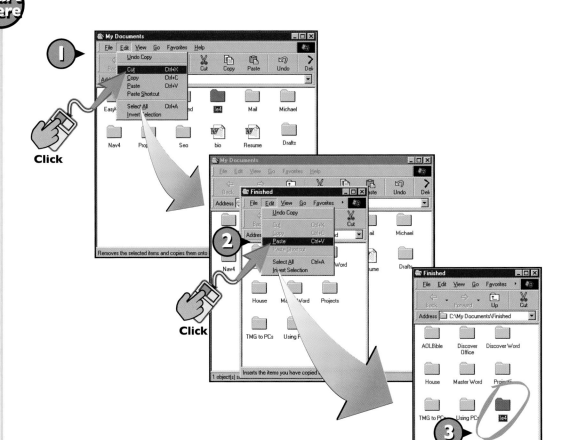

Start Here

Click

Click

✓ **Undo Move**
You can select the **Undo** command from the **Edit** menu to undo the move if you change your mind.

✓ **Move by Dragging**
You can move a folder by opening both the window containing the folder (the source) and the window to which you will move the folder (the destination). Then press and hold the **Shift** key and drag the folder from the source window to the destination window.

 After you select the folder you want to move, click **Edit** and then select the **Cut** command.

 Open the drive or folder window where you want the folder to be moved. Click **Edit**, and then select the **Paste** command.

 Windows moves the folder to the new location.

End Task

Task 11: Renaming Folders

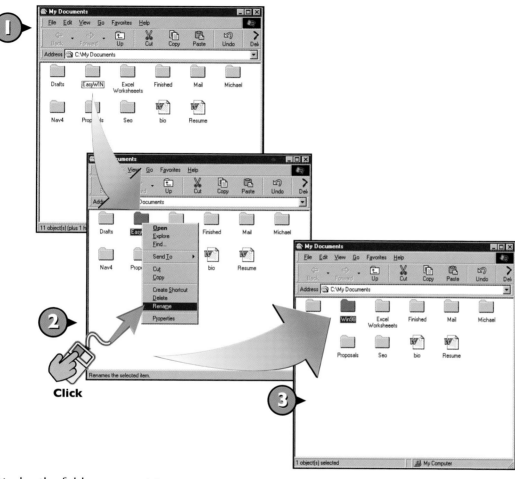

Click

As you add more and more folders and files to your computer, you will eventually need to rearrange and reorganize them. In addition to needing to know how to move folders, you'll need to know how to rename them (for instance, in case you want to give a folder a more descriptive name). Fortunately, Windows 98 lets you easily rename folders.

✅ **Folder Names**
Folder names and filenames can contain as many as 255 characters, including spaces. You also can include letters, numbers, and other symbols on your keyboard, except the following:

| ? / : " * < > \

✅ **Single-Click Renaming**
Click the folder once to select it, and then single-click within the name to edit the name.

1 ▶ Display the folder you want to rename.

2 ▶ Right-click the folder, click the **Rename** command in the shortcut dialog, type a new name for the folder, and press **Enter**.

3 ▶ The folder is renamed.

End Task

Task 12: Deleting Folders

You can delete folders when you no longer need them. When you delete a folder from your hard drive, you also delete its contents. Windows 98 places deleted folders in the **Recycle Bin**. You can restore deleted items from the **Recycle Bin** if you realize you have placed items there by accident.

✅ Shortcuts
You can right-click the folder and choose the **Delete** command or click the **Delete** button in the toolbar.

✅ Cancel Deletion
If you change your mind about deleting the folder, click the **No** button in the **Confirm Folder Delete** dialog box. Alternatively, undo the deletion by selecting the **Edit Undo** command.

✅ Be Careful!
When you delete a folder from a floppy drive, that item does not land in the **Recycle Bin**; it is immediately deleted from your system.

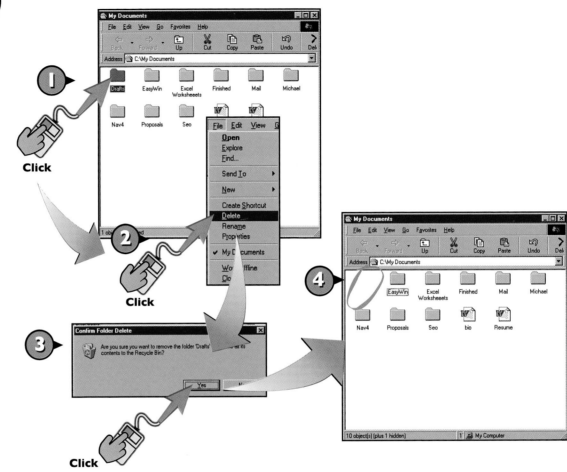

1. Select the folder you want to delete.

2. Click **File**, and then select the **Delete** command.

3. Click the **Yes** button.

4. The folder is deleted.

Task 13: Selecting a Single File

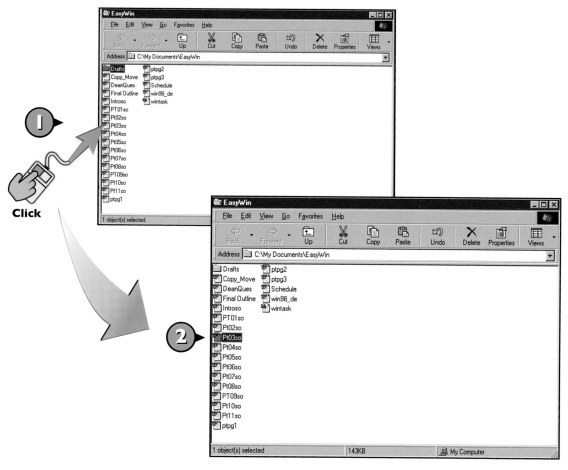

When you want to work on files (copy, move, print, delete, and so on), you start by selecting the files you want. Selecting a single file is simple.

Click

1 ▶ Click the file you want to work with.

2 ▶ That file is selected.

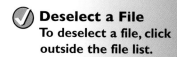
Deselect a File
To deselect a file, click outside the file list.

Task 14: Selecting Multiple Files That Are Next to Each Other

Windows 98 enables you to easily select multiple files that are grouped together in the folder.

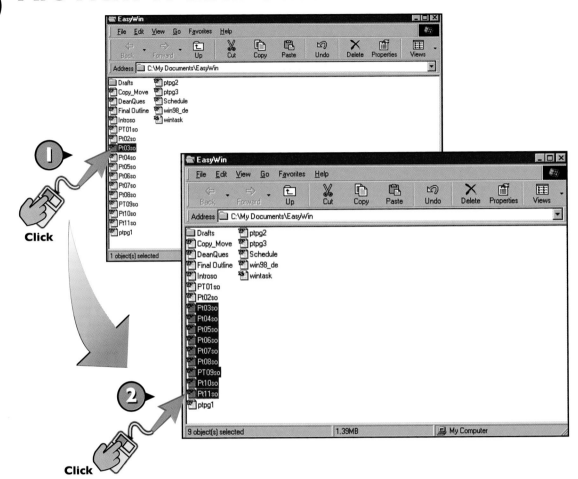

Click

Click

✓ **Select Folders**
You can select a group of folders using this same method.

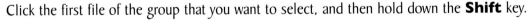

1 Click the first file of the group that you want to select, and then hold down the **Shift** key.

2 Click the last file in the group that you want to select; the first and last files, as well as all the files in between, are selected.

Task 15: Selecting Multiple Files That Are Not Next to Each Other

Start Here

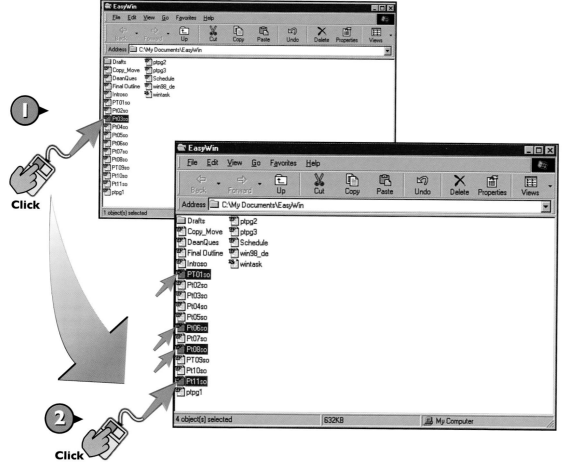

Click

Click

Even if the files you want to select are not grouped together, you can still select them using Windows 98.

✓ **Select a File by Mistake?**
If you select a file by mistake, you can Ctrl-Click the file again to deselect it.

1 ▶ Click the first file that you want to select, and hold down the **Ctrl** key.

2 ▶ While holding down the **Ctrl** key, click each file that you want to select. Each file you click remains selected.

End Task

Page
77

PART 3

Task 16: Selecting All Files

Windows 98 enables you to easily select all the files in a window.

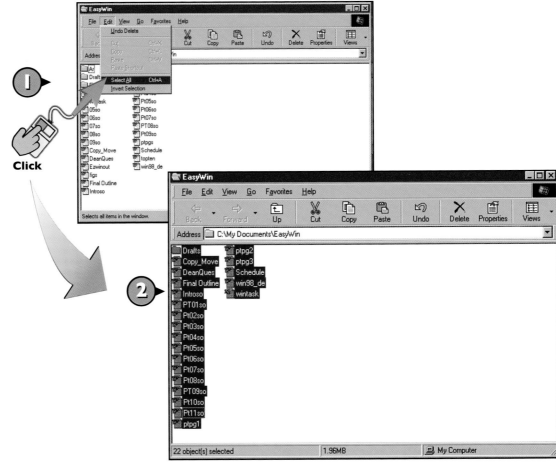

Click

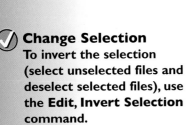

Change Selection
To invert the selection (select unselected files and deselect selected files), use the **Edit, Invert Selection** command.

1 ▶ Click **Edit**, and then click the **Select All** command.

2 ▶ All files are selected.

Task 17: Copying a File to Another Folder

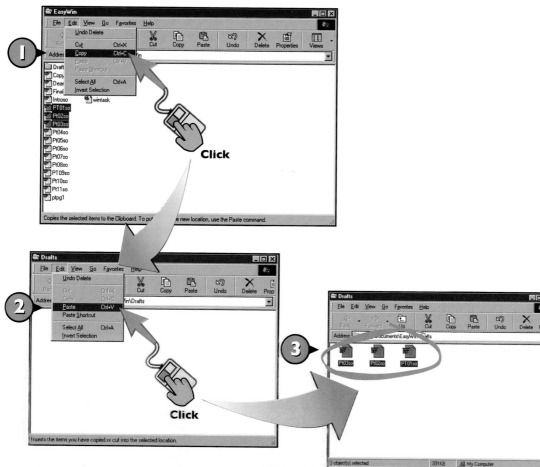

Windows makes it easy to copy files from one folder to another and from one disk to another. You might copy files in order to create a backup copy or to revise one copy while keeping the original file intact.

Click

Click

① Select the file(s) you want to copy. Click **Edit**, and then select the **Copy** command.

② Open the folder to which you want to paste the copied file(s), click **Edit**, and then select the **Paste** command.

③ Windows copies the file(s) to the new location.

✓ Drag-and-Drop Copying

To use drag-and-drop editing to copy files, open both the window that contains the file (source) and the window for the folder or drive to which you want to copy the file (destination). Hold the Ctrl key and drag the file to its destination.

✓ Shortcuts

Alternatively, you can click the **Copy** button or right-click and select **Copy** from the shortcut menu.

Task 18: Copying a File to a Floppy Disk

You might want to copy a file to a floppy disk to take the file with you or to make a backup copy. Windows provides a shortcut (the **Send To** command) for copying a file to a floppy disk.

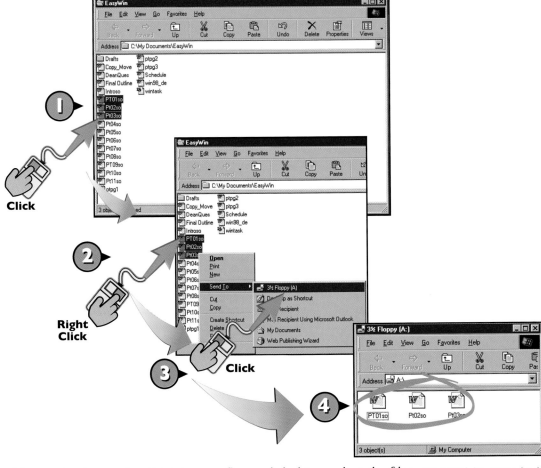

Click

Right Click

Click

✓ **Disk Full?**
If the disk is full, you see an error message. Insert a different disk and click the **Retry** button.

1 After you've inserted a disk into your floppy disk drive, select the files you want to copy to the disk.

2 Right-click the selected files.

3 Select the **Send To** command from the shortcut menu, and choose the appropriate floppy drive.

4 The files are copied to that disk.

End Task

Task 19: Moving a File

 Start Here

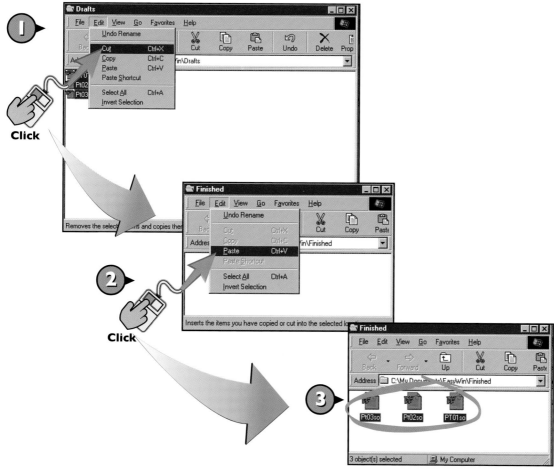

Click

Click

You might need to move files from one folder or drive to another (for example, in order to reorganize folders by putting similar files together in the same folder). You might also move a file that you accidentally saved in the wrong folder.

✓ **Undo Move**
If you make a mistake, you can undo the move by selecting the **Undo** command from the **Edit** menu.

✓ **Drag to Move**
You can also drag a file to a different folder. Open the window that contains the file and the window for the folder or drive to which you want to move the file. If you are moving from one folder to another, simply drag the file(s) from one window to the other. If you are moving from one drive to another, hold down the **Shift** key and drag.

① Select the file(s) you want to move, click **Edit**, and then select the **Cut** command.

② Open the folder or drive to which you want to paste the file(s), click **Edit**, and then select the **Paste** command.

③ Windows moves the files to the new location.

 End Task

Task 20: Deleting a File

Eventually, your computer will become full of files, and you'll have a hard time organizing and storing them all. You can copy necessary files to floppy disks, tapes, and so on, and then delete the files from your hard drive to make room for new files. In addition, you will sometimes want to delete files you no longer need.

✅ Undo the Deletion
You can undo a deletion by selecting the **Undo** command from the **Edit** menu. Alternatively, you can retrieve the deleted item from the **Recycle Bin**, as covered in the next task.

✅ Delete Shortcuts
Other alternatives for deleting files and folders include clicking the **Delete** button, right-clicking the folder or file and choosing **Delete** from the shortcut menu, and pressing the **Delete** key on your keyboard.

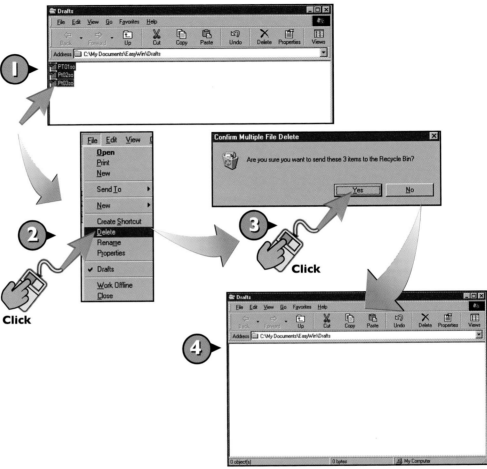

Click

Click

Click

1. Select the file(s) you want to delete.

2. Click **File**, and then select the **Delete** command.

3. Click **Yes** to delete the file(s).

4. Windows removes the file(s), placing it in the **Recycle Bin**.

Task 21: Undeleting a File or Folder

Start Here

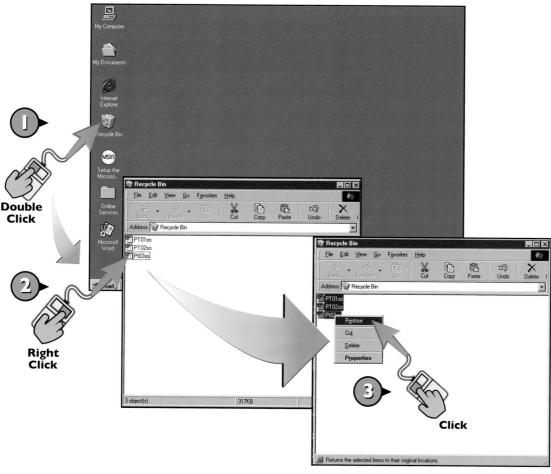

① Double Click

② Right Click

③ Click

Sometimes you will delete a file or folder by mistake. You can retrieve the file or folder from the **Recycle Bin** (as long as the **Recycle Bin** has not been emptied) and return it to its original location.

① ▶ Double-click the **Recycle Bin** icon.

② ▶ In the **Recycle Bin** window, you see the contents of all the files, programs, and folders you have deleted. Select and then right-click the file(s) or folder(s) you want to undelete.

③ ▶ Select the **Restore** command from the shortcut menu. The file(s) or folder(s) is moved from the **Recycle Bin** to its original location.

✅ **Clean Out Recycle Bin**
If you want to be permanently rid of the files in the **Recycle Bin**, you can empty it. Double-click the **Recycle Bin** icon and make sure that it doesn't contain anything you need to save. Then choose the **Empty Recycle Bin** command from the **File** menu. Windows displays the **Confirm Multiple File Delete** dialog box; click **Yes** to empty the **Recycle Bin**.

End Task

Task 22: Creating a Shortcut to a File or Folder

If you often use the same file or folder, you might want fast access to it. If so, you can create a shortcut icon for the file or folder on the desktop. Double-clicking a file's shortcut icon opens the file in the program you used to create the file. Double-clicking a folder displays the contents of the folder in a window.

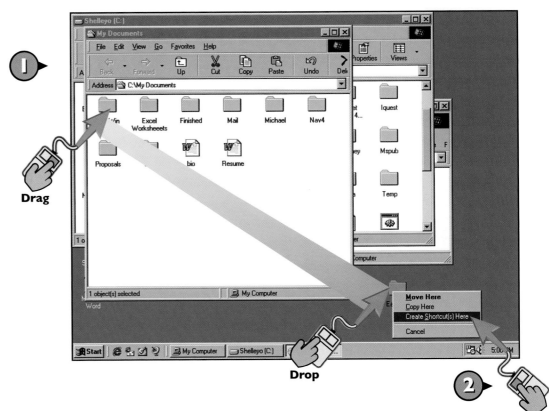

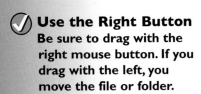

✓ **Use the Right Button**
Be sure to drag with the right mouse button. If you drag with the left, you move the file or folder.

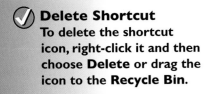

✓ **Delete Shortcut**
To delete the shortcut icon, right-click it and then choose **Delete** or drag the icon to the **Recycle Bin**.

 After you open the folder or drive containing the file for which you want to create a shortcut icon, press the right mouse button and drag the folder or file icon to your desktop.

 Right click the icon on the desktop and select the **Create Shortcut(s) Here** command.

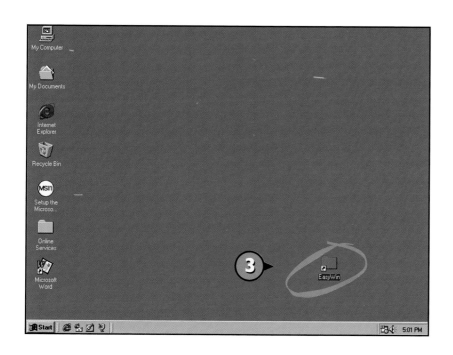

 Windows adds a shortcut icon to your desktop. (You can close the other windows to better see the shortcut icon, as I've done here).

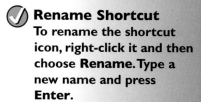 **Rename Shortcut**
To rename the shortcut icon, right-click it and then choose **Rename.** Type a new name and press **Enter.**

Task 23: Finding Files and Folders

After you've worked for months with your applications, your computer will become filled with various folders and files, which can make it nearly impossible for you to know where everything is. Luckily, Windows includes a command that helps you locate specific files or folders by name, file type, location, and so on.

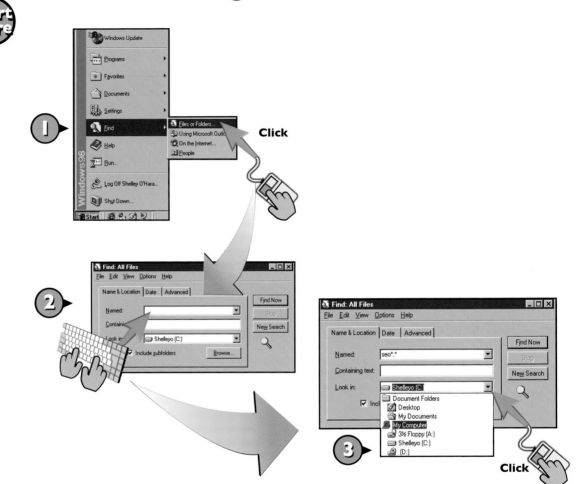

Click

Wild Card Searching
You can use the characters * and ? (known as *wildcards*) in the search. For example, to find all files ending with the extension **.doc**, you could type *.doc. Similarly, you could type **chap??.*** to find all files beginning with **chap**, followed by any two characters, and ending in any extension.

1 ▶ Click the **Start** button, select the **Find** command, and then choose **Files or Folders**.

2 ▶ Enter the name of the file you want to search for.

3 ▶ To change the drive on which Windows will conduct the search, display the **Look in** list box and choose the floppy or CD-ROM drive from the drop-down list.

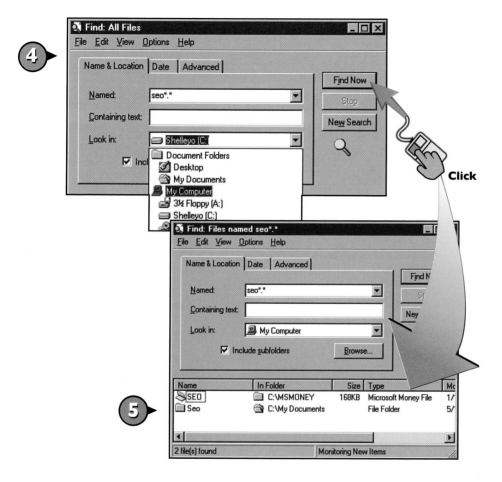

Click

(4) Click the **Find Now** button.

(5) Windows searches the hard drive by default and displays a list of found files at the bottom of the dialog box. You can double-click any of the listed files or folders to go to that file or folder.

✅ **Other Options**
If you do not know the name of the file but you know what type of file it is, click the **Advanced** tab in the **Find** dialog box. From the **Of type** list box, choose the type of file you're searching for (such as **Application, Configuration, Help, Microsoft Word Document,** or **Text Document**). Click the **Find Now** button, and Windows performs the search.

Task 24: Using Windows Explorer

You can use **Windows Explorer** in much the same way you use the **My Computer** window: to copy and move folders, to create and rename folders, to view details, and so on. You might be more comfortable using Explorer if you have used Windows 3.0 or 3.1 because the Explorer in Windows 98 is very similar to the File Manager in previous versions of Windows. Alternatively, you might simply prefer the appearance of Windows Explorer to that of the **My Computer** window.

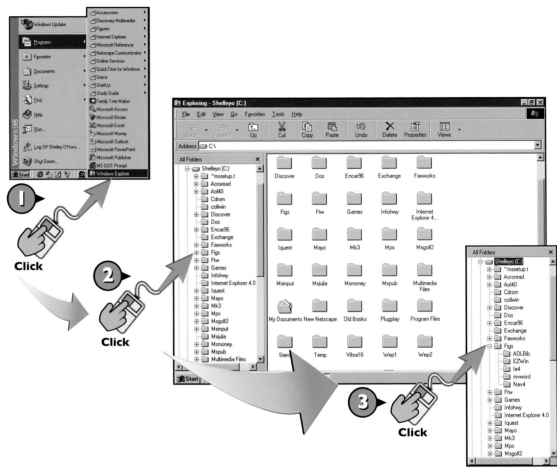

Click

Click

Click

✔ **Close Program**
Close Windows Explorer just like you do any other program: Select the **Exit** command from the **File** menu or click the **Close** button in the program's title bar.

1 ▶ Click the **Start** button, select the **Programs** command, and choose **Windows Explorer**.

2 ▶ To display folders within a folder, click the plus sign.

3 ▶ The list expands to show other folders. A minus sign appears next to the folder name. To hide a folder, click the minus sign.

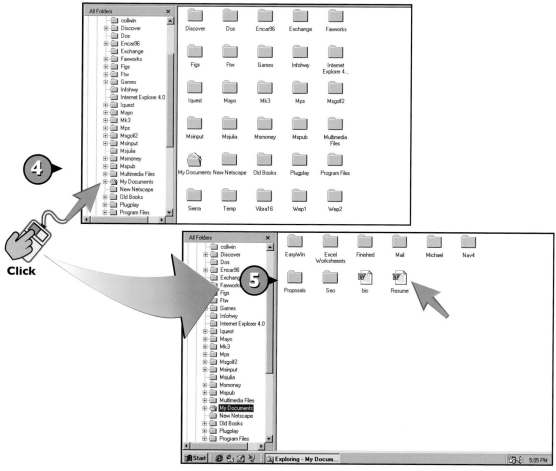

Click

4 To display a folder's contents, click the folder in the list in the left pane.

5 The folder's contents appear on the right side of the Explorer window.

Move and Copying
You can use any of the commands and features of Windows Explorer to move, copy, delete, and work with files and folders. One thing that is easy to do with Explorer is to copy and move files by dragging. Drag a file from the right side of the Explorer window to the left side and drop it on top of the folder you want to copy or move it to. When you drag a file to another drive, Windows copies the file; when you drag the file to another folder, Windows moves it.

Left Side
The left side of the split Explorer window lists all drives and folders on the hard drive. The right side displays the folders and files in the selected folder or drive on the left.

Plus Sign
Any folder with a plus sign in front of it contains more folders and files.

End Task

Printing with Windows

All Windows applications use the same setup for your printer, which saves time and ensures that you can print from any Windows application without resetting for each program. When you first install Windows, it sets up your printer. If needed, you can set up more than one printer in Windows and choose the printer you want to use at any given time. In addition, you can easily manage printing for all of your applications through Windows.

You print a document from the application in which you created it. When you send a file to the printer, the file first goes to a *print queue*, or holding area. The print queue can contain one or many files at any time, and you can make changes to this print queue. While a file is in the print queue, you can pause, restart, and even cancel the printing. This part shows you how to control and manage printing in Windows.

Tasks

Task 1: Previewing a Document

In most applications, you can preview a document to check the margins, heads, graphic placement, and so on before you print.

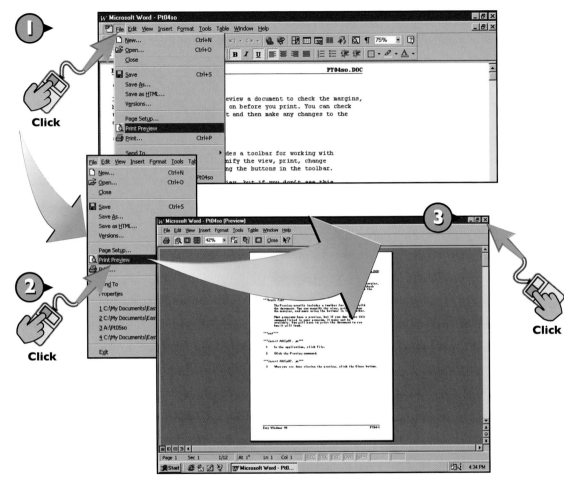

Start Here

Click

Click

Click

✓ **Toolbar**
The **Print Preview** view usually includes a toolbar for working with the document. Using buttons in this toolbar, you can magnify the view, print, change the margins, and more.

✓ **No Preview?**
Most programs have a preview option, but if you don't see this command listed in your program, it might not be available. You will have to print the document to see how it looks.

 Click **File**.

 Select the **Print Preview** command.

 After you finish viewing the preview, click the **Close** button.

Task 2: Printing a Document

Start Here

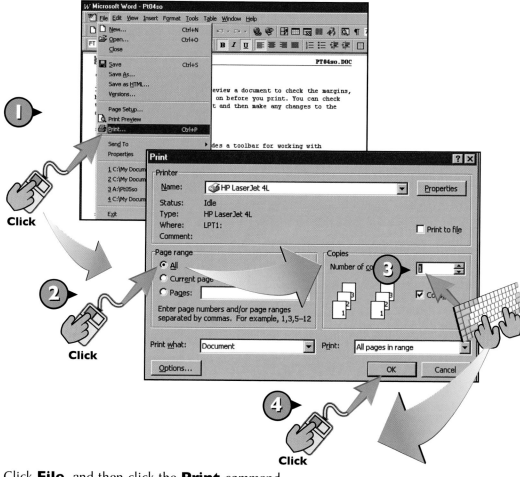

Click

Click

Click

When you first install Windows, it sets up a primary printer, and you can print from any application using this printer. Printing your documents gives you a paper copy you can proof-read, use in reports, give to co-workers, and so on.

✓ **Shortcut**
As a shortcut, use the **Print** button in your toolbar. Alternatively, you can use a keyboard shortcut (usually **Ctrl+P**) to print.

✓ **Use Another Printer**
If you want to use a printer other than the default, choose the printer you want to use from the **Name** drop-down list in the **Print** dialog box.

✓ **See Printer Details**
Click the **Properties** button to display a dialog box specific to the selected printer. From this dialog box, choose the paper size, page orientation, specifics about printing graphics, and so on.

① ▶ Click **File**, and then click the **Print** command.

② ▶ In the **Print** dialog, specify a page range.

③ ▶ Enter the number of copies you want printed.

④ ▶ Click the **OK** button.

End Task

Task 3: Viewing the Print Queue

The print queue lists the documents that have been set to a printer, and it shows how far along the printing is. Using the print queue, you can pause, restart, or cancel print jobs. This task shows how to view the print queue.

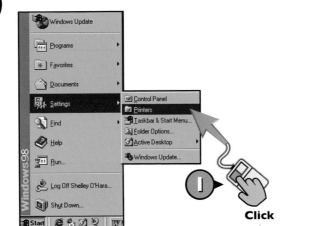

Start Here

Click

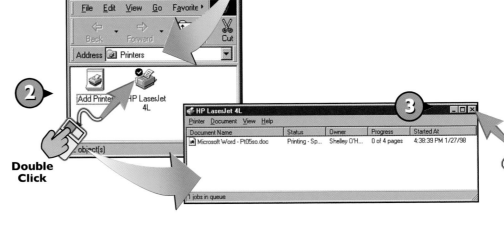

Double Click

Click

Close Window
To close the print queue, click the **Close** button.

Double-Click Icon
You can display the print queue by double-clicking the **Printer** icon in the taskbar. This icon appears whenever you are printing something.

Empty?
If the print queue window is empty, there is nothing in the print queue.

1. Click the **Start** button, click the **Settings** command, and then choose **Printers**.

2. Double-click the printer whose print queue you want to view.

3. The printer window displays a list of the documents in the queue as well as statistics about the documents being printed. Click the **Close** button to close the queue.

End Task

Task 4: Pausing and Restarting the Printer

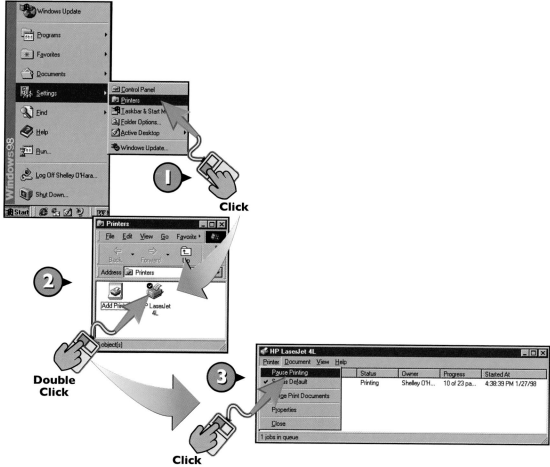

You might want to pause printing when you have to make a change in the text or when you want to load a different paper type. You can easily stop the printing from the **Printers** folder, and can restart it at any time.

✅ Nothing Listed?
You have to be quick to pause or stop a short print job. If nothing appears in the print queue, it probably means that the entire print job has already been sent to the printer.

✅ Pause a Job
You can use the **Document** menu in the print queue to pause printing on a specific job (if, for example, you have sent several jobs to the printer but want to pause and change paper for a particular job). Select the job you want to pause and choose the **Pause Printing** command from the **Document** menu. To restart the printer after you have paused it, click **Printer** and then click the **Pause Printing** command again.

1 Click the **Start** button, click the **Settings** command, and then choose **Printers**.

2 Double-click the printer whose print queue you want to view.

3 Click **Printer**, and then select the **Pause Printing** command.

Task 5: Canceling Printing

If you discover an error in the job you are printing or if you decide that you need to add something to it, you can cancel the print job. Canceling the print job prevents you from wasting time and paper.

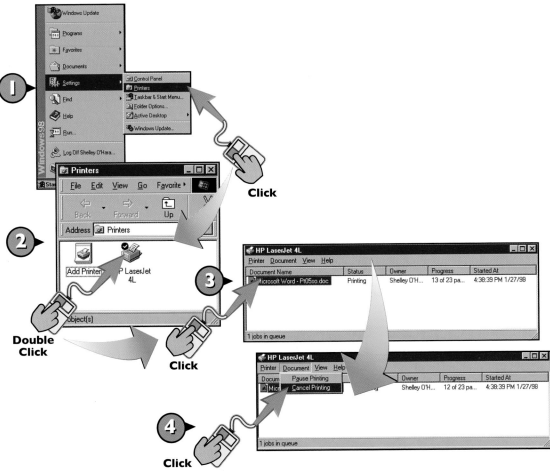

Click

Double Click

Click

Click

Click

✓ **Nothing Listed?**
Depending on your computer and your printer, the print job might be listed in the print queue for only a few seconds before it is sent to the printer. You might not be able to cancel it.

1 ▶ Click the **Start** button, click the **Settings** command, and then select **Printers**.

2 ▶ Double-click the printer whose print queue you want to view.

3 ▶ In the print queue, select the print job you want to cancel.

4 ▶ Click **Document**, and then select the **Cancel Printing** command.

End Task

Task 6: Setting the Default Printer

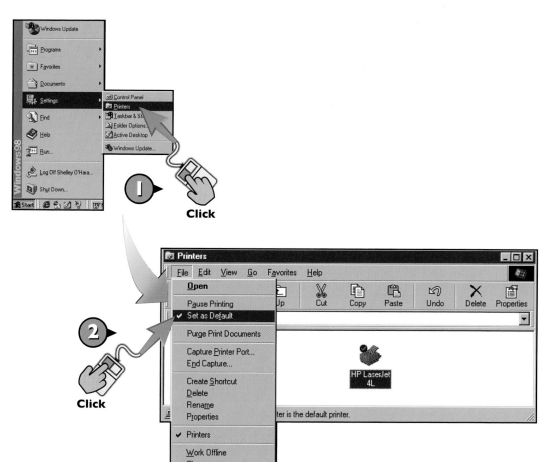

Click

Click

If you have more than one printer connected, you must select one as the default. The default printer you set in Windows is the printer your applications automatically use when you choose to print. The default printer is the one you want most of your documents printed on.

1 ▶ Click the **Start** button, click **Settings**, and then select the **Printers** command.

2 ▶ After you select the printer you want to choose as the default, click **File**, and then select the **Set as Default** command.

 Change Default
To use a different printer, follow this same procedure, but select the new printer you want to use as the default.

Task 7: Changing Printer Settings

You can easily change printer settings. You might, for example, switch to a new printer driver so that your printer works better with your applications; alternatively, you might change the port to which your printer connects to make room for another external device, such as a modem or tape drive.

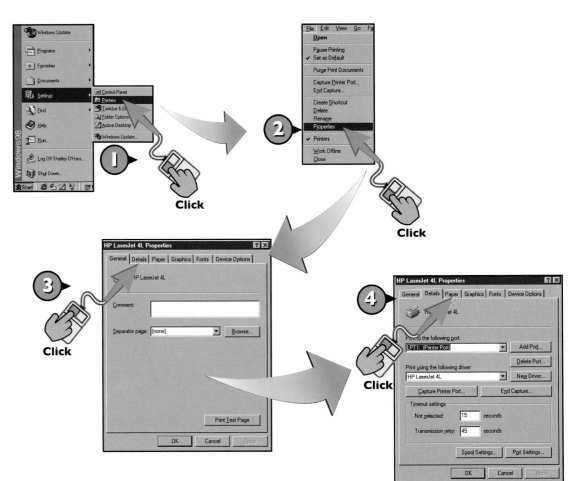

Start Here

Click

Click

Click

Click

✓ **Port Selection**
Use the drop-down list to select from common ports. Choose which driver to use from that drop-down list, or click the **New Driver** button to install a new driver.

1 ▶ Click the **Start** button, click the **Settings** command, and then choose **Printers**.

2 ▶ After you select the printer you want to modify, click **File**, and then select the **Properties** command.

3 ▶ Click the **Details** tab.

4 ▶ Make the necessary changes to the printer port, driver, timeout settings, and so on. After you finish, click the **Paper** tab.

Next Step ▶

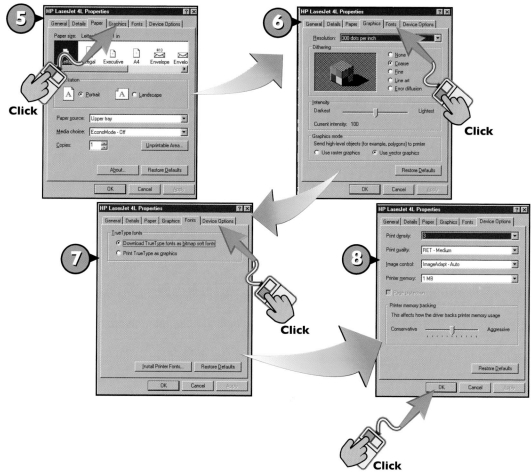

Click

Click

Click

Click

✅ **Change for One Job**
Changing the printer's properties changes them for all documents you print on this printer. If you want to change properties for just one document, use the **Page Settings** or **Print Setup** command in the particular program.

✅ **Restore Defaults**
If you make a change in the **Paper**, **Graphics**, **Fonts**, or **Device Options** tab and change your mind about the changes, you can choose the **Restore Defaults** button in that tab to cancel just that tab's changes.

✅ **Options Vary**
The number and titles of tab settings in the **Properties** dialog will vary depending on the type of printer you have.

✅ **What's Timeout?**
Timeout settings specify how long Windows will wait before reporting an error to you.

5 ▶ Make changes to the paper size, orientation, source, number of copies, and other options. After you finish, click the **Graphics** tab.

6 ▶ Make changes to the print resolution, dithering, shading intensity, and graphics mode. After you finish, click the **Fonts** tab.

7 ▶ Install printer fonts or new font cartridges. Choose any font cartridge you have added to enable the use of its fonts in Windows. After you finish, click the **Device Options** tab.

8 ▶ Use the **Device Options** tab to choose printed text quality; the available options depend on your printer. After you finish, click the **OK** button.

End Task

Task 8: Adding a Printer

You can add a new printer to your Windows setup using a step-by-step guide called a *wizard* that Windows provides. Use the wizard any time you get a new printer or change printers.

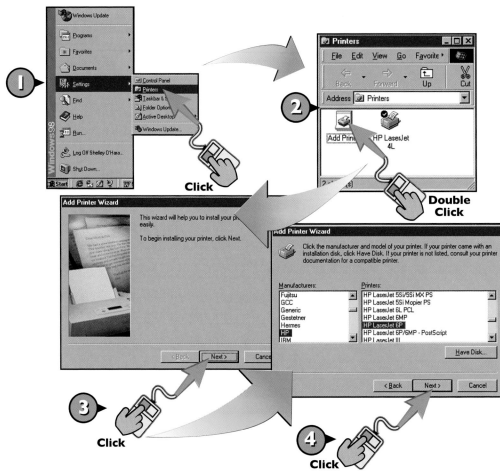

Click

Double Click

Click

Click

Next Step

✅ **Cancel**
You can cancel this process at any time by clicking the **Cancel** button in any of the wizard dialog boxes.

✅ **Go Back a Step**
Click the **Back** button in a wizard dialog box to return to the previous dialog and review or modify your selections.

1 ▸ Click the **Start** button, click the **Settings** command, and then select **Printers**.

2 ▸ Double-click the **Add Printer** icon.

3 ▸ Click the **Next** button to continue with the installation.

4 ▸ Select the name of your printer's manufacturer from the **Manufacturers** list box, select the appropriate printer from the **Printers** list box, and then click **Next**.

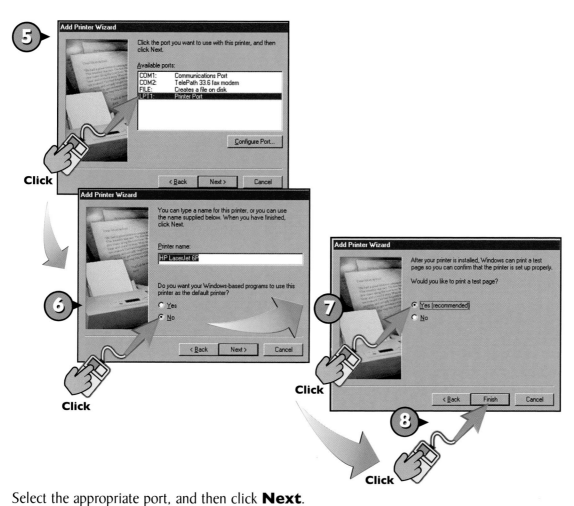

Click

Click

Click

Click

Click

Page
101

⑤ ▶ Select the appropriate port, and then click **Next**.

⑥ ▶ Enter a name for the printer, or accept the one Windows has given it, and then select whether you want the new printer to be the default printer. After you finish, click **Next**.

⑦ ▶ Click the **Yes** radio button to print a test page.

⑧ ▶ Click the **Finish** button. Windows adds the new printer's icon to the **Printers** folder.

✅ **Use Disk**
If you want to use drivers supplied by your printer manufacturer, click the **Have Disk** button instead of clicking **Next**. Insert the appropriate disk and follow the onscreen instructions.

✅ **Test Page**
If you select **Yes** to print a test page, Windows prints a test page, and you are asked whether it printed successfully.

End
Task

Task 9: Deleting a Printer

If you get a new printer, you can delete the setup for the old printer so that you don't get confused about which printer is which. Deleting a printer removes it from the available list of printers.

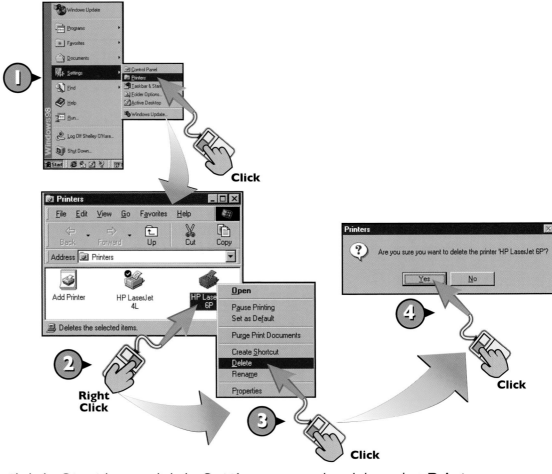

Undo Deletion
If you delete a printer by mistake, you can always add it back using the **Add Printer** wizard (refer to the preceding task).

1. Click the **Start** button, click the **Settings** command, and then select **Printers**.

2. Right-click the printer you want to delete.

3. Select the **Delete** command from the shortcut menu.

4. Click the **Yes** button to confirm the deletion.

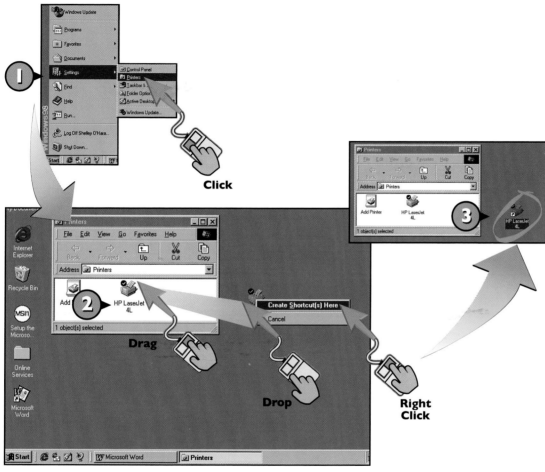

Click

Drag

Drop

Right Click

For fast access to your printer, you can add a printer icon to your desktop. You can then double-click this icon to view the print queue. You can also drag documents from a file window to the printer icon to print the documents.

✓ Wrong Button?
If you drag with the left mouse button, you see a message telling you that you cannot copy the icon to the desktop. You are asked whether you want to create a shortcut icon instead. Click the **Yes** button to create a shortcut icon.

✓ Delete Icon
To delete the shortcut icon, right-click it and then select **Delete** from the shortcut menu. When prompted to confirm the deletion, click the **Yes** button.

1 ▶ Click the **Start** button, click the **Settings** command, and then select **Printers**.

2 ▶ With the right mouse button, drag your printer icon from the **Printer** folder to your desktop, and then click the **Create Shortcut(s) Here** command.

3 ▶ The printer shortcut is added to your desktop.

Task 11: Viewing Fonts

The fonts you can select to use in a document depend on the fonts installed on your system. You can view a list of fonts and see an example of any of the available fonts.

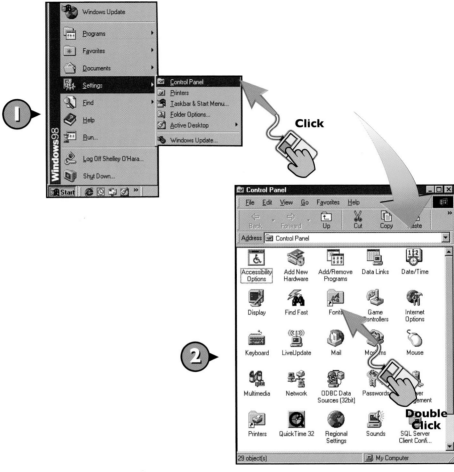

Click

Double Click

✓ **View list**
You can view the fonts by list rather than by icon. To do so, click the **List** button in the toolbar. Alternatively, open the **View** menu and select **List**. You can also view similar fonts by clicking **Similarity**.

① Click the **Start** button, choose **Settings**, and select **Control Panel**.

② Double-click the **Fonts** icon.

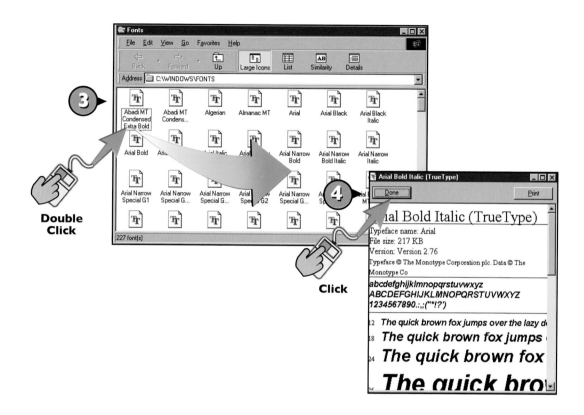

**Double
Click**

Click

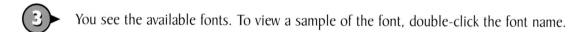

③ ► You see the available fonts. To view a sample of the font, double-click the font name.

④ ► Click the **Done** button.

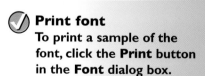

Print font
**To print a sample of the
font, click the Print button
in the Font dialog box.**

Task 12: Adding Fonts

You can purchase additional fonts to add to your system. When you do so, you can install them in Windows so that you can use them with any Windows programs.

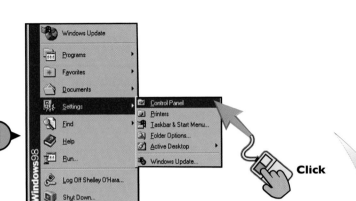

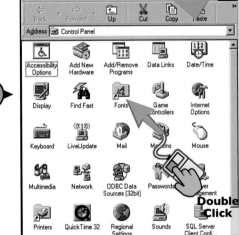

Another drive?
If the fonts are on another drive, select that drive from the **Drives** drop-down list.

No fonts listed?
If no fonts are listed, it's because there are no font files in the selected folder. Be sure to select the drive and folder where the files are stored.

 Click the **Start** button, choose **Settings**, and select **Control Panel**.

 Double-click the **Fonts** icon.

Next Step

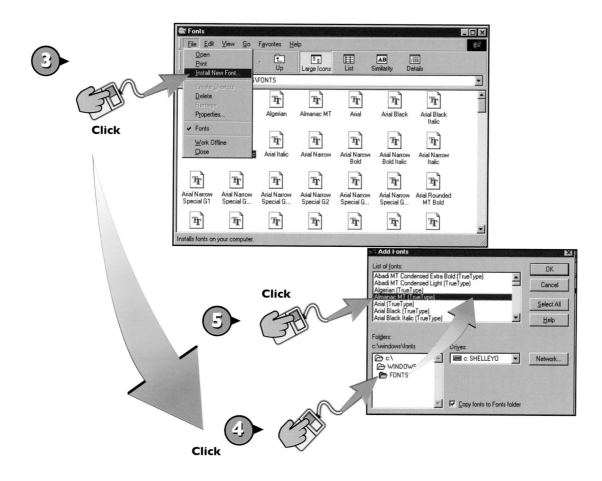

Click

Click

Click

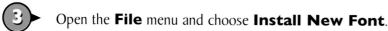

3 ▶ Open the **File** menu and choose **Install New Font**.

4 ▶ Select the folder where the font is stored.

5 ▶ Select the font(s) you want to install, and then click **OK**. The font is installed.

✓ **Select all fonts**
To select all the fonts, click the **Select All** button.

PART 5

Personalizing Windows

To make Windows most suited to how you work, Microsoft has made it easy for you to customize the program. You can move and resize the taskbar, placing it where you like on the desktop. You can adjust the colors used for onscreen elements such as the title bar. You can change how the mouse works, when sounds are played, and more. Windows 98 includes many options for setting up your work environment just the way you want. This part shows you how to customize Windows.

Tasks

Task 1: Showing and Hiding the Taskbar

Windows' default is to show the taskbar at all times on the desktop. You can, however, hide the taskbar so that you have more room on the desktop for other windows, folders, and programs. When you hide the taskbar, it disappears while you are working in a window and then reappears when you move the mouse to the bottom of the screen.

✓ **Undo Change**
To undo this change, open the **Start** menu, click the **Settings** command, and then click **Taskbar & Start Menu**. Click the **Auto Hide** option to remove the check mark. Then click **OK**.

✓ **Right-Click**
You can right-click a blank area of the taskbar and select **Properties** to make a change.

✓ **Use Small Icons**
You can select to display small icons and to enable or disable the clock.

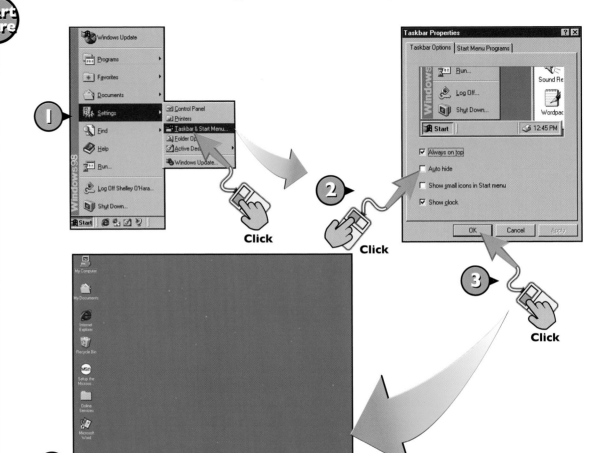

1 Click **Start**, click the **Settings** command, and then select **Taskbar & Start Menu**.

2 Click the **Auto hide** check box.

3 Click the **OK** button.

4 The dialog closes, and the taskbar disappears.

Task 2: Moving the Taskbar

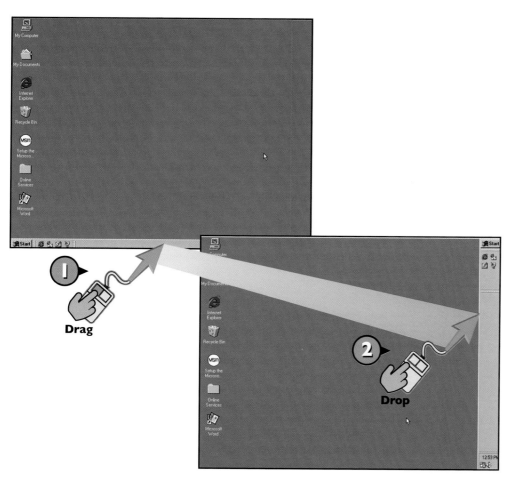

Drag

Drop

Windows enables you to place the taskbar on the top, left, right, or bottom of the screen so that the desktop is set up how you like it. Try moving the taskbar to various areas on the screen, and then choose the area you like best.

Position the mouse pointer anywhere on the taskbar except on a button or the clock. Press and hold the left mouse button and drag the taskbar to the location you want.

When you release the mouse button, the taskbar jumps to the new location.

 Move Back
To move the taskbar back to the bottom of the screen, drag it to that area.

Task 3: Resizing the Taskbar

In addition to moving the taskbar, you can also resize it (for example, making it larger so that the buttons are bigger and easier to read). You resize the taskbar just as you resize a window—by dragging its border.

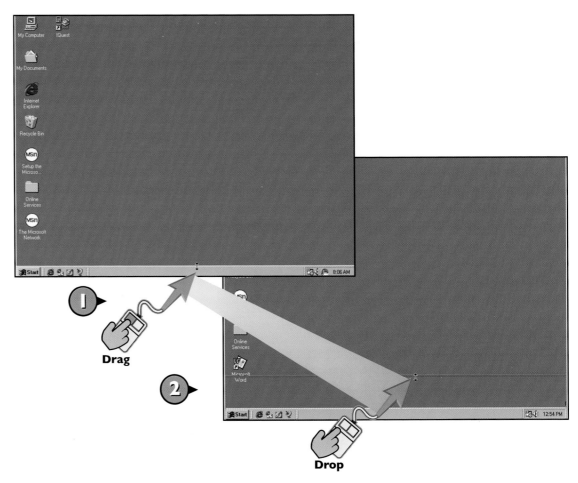

Drag

Drop

✓ **Undo Size**
Follow this same procedure to change the size back.

 Position the mouse pointer on one of the taskbar's borders. The pointer should look like a double-headed arrow.

 Drag the arrow to resize the taskbar.

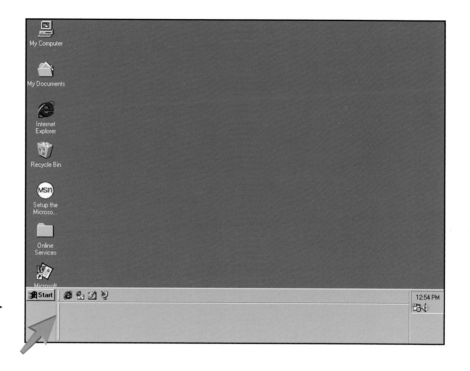

3 After you release the mouse button, the taskbar is resized.

Task 4: Using Wallpaper for the Desktop

You can personalize your desktop in Windows by adding wallpaper. Windows offers many colorful wallpaper options, including cars, honeycombs, squares, zigzags, and more.

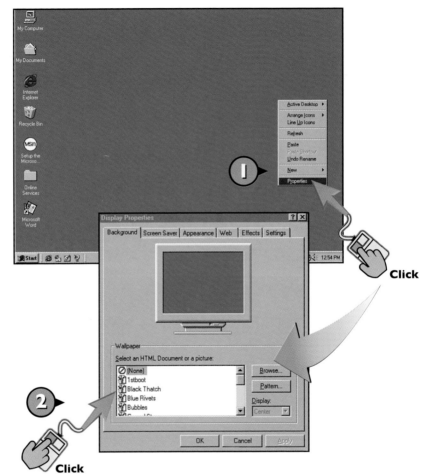

Click

Click

✔ Use a Pattern
You can also add a pattern to the desktop as covered in the next task.

✔ Wallpaper Centered?
If you see only one small image in the center of your screen when selecting a wallpaper, click the **Display** drop-down list and choose **Tile**. Click **Apply**, and then click **OK** to accept the changes.

 Right-click any blank area of the desktop, and then click **Properties**.

 Select the wallpaper you want displayed on your desktop (use the scrollbars if necessary).

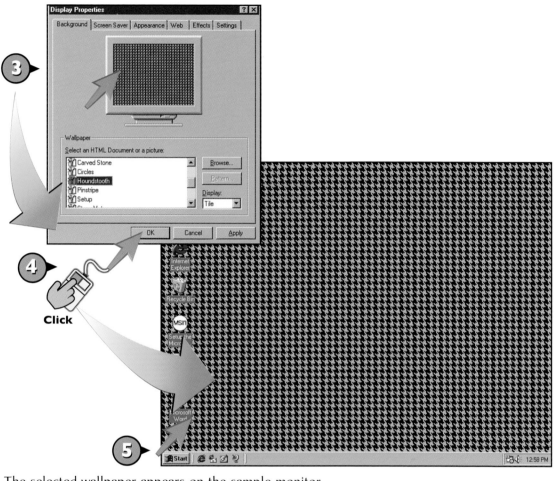

Click

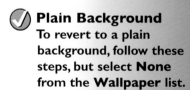

3 The selected wallpaper appears on the sample monitor.

4 Click the **OK** button.

5 The wallpaper is added to your desktop background.

✓ **Plain Background**
To revert to a plain background, follow these steps, but select **None** from the **Wallpaper** list.

Task 5: Using a Pattern for the Desktop

If you don't like the wallpaper selections, you might want to experiment with a pattern. A pattern consists of a pattern of dots repeated in the screen colors. Wallpaper is an image that can have different colors. Windows offers paisley, tulip, waffle, and box background patterns (among others).

✓ **Computer Slower?**
Using wallpaper and patterns generally slows the speed of your computer and taxes its memory. If your applications seem too slow or if you decide you don't want a pattern or wallpaper, return to the **Display Properties** dialog box, click the **Patterns** button, and choose **(None)**.

✓ **Wallpaper or Pattern**
You cannot use both a wallpaper and a pattern. If you select a wallpaper, the **Pattern** button is dimmed. If you want to use a pattern, select **None** from the **Wallpaper** list.

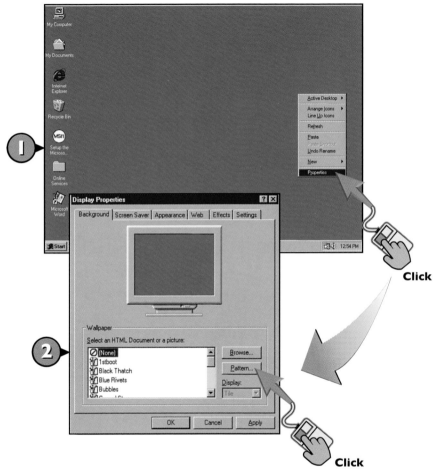

Click

Click

1 ▶ Right-click any blank area of the desktop, and then click **Properties**.

2 ▶ Click the **Pattern** button.

Next Step

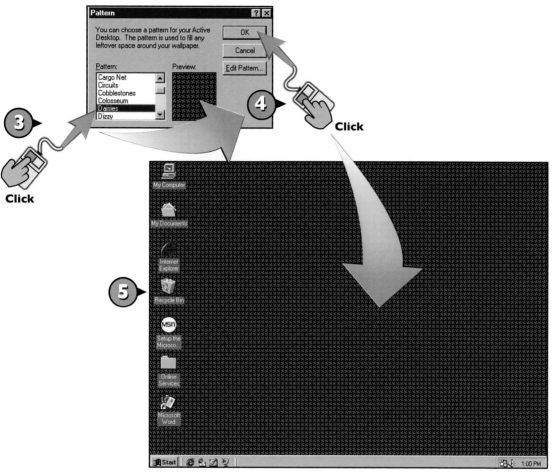

Click

Click

3 ▶ Select the pattern you want displayed on your desktop. The selected pattern appears in the **Preview** area.

4 ▶ Click the **OK** button to use this pattern and to close the **Pattern** dialog box.

5 ▶ Windows uses the selected pattern on your desktop.

✓ **Create Your Own Pattern**
You can create your own pattern. Click a pattern and then click Edit Pattern. Click the boxes in the pattern to edit the shape of the pattern. Click Done.

End Task

If you want to use something different for the background, consider using a Web page. You can select any Web page you have saved on your system.

 **Use Any Background File**

You can use any type of HTML or picture file as the background. Simply change to the drive and folder and select the background file you want to use.

 Not Linked

Keep in mind that the Web page is not linked to the content of that specific Web page, but is a static image.

Task 6: Using a Web Page As Your Windows Background

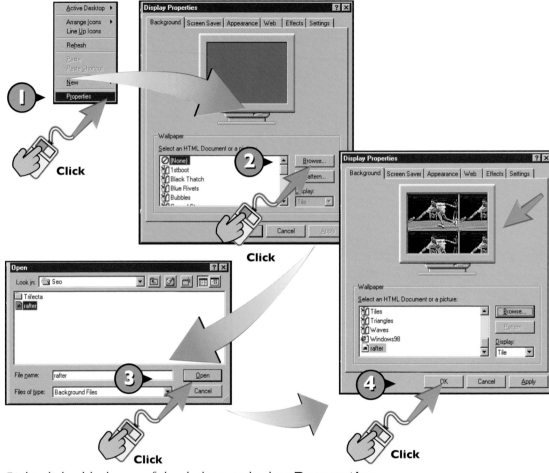

Click

Click

Click

Click

① ▶ Right-click a blank area of the desktop and select **Properties**.

② ▶ On the **Background** tab, click the **Browse** button.

③ ▶ Navigate to the drive and folder where the image is stored, click the image file, and click **Open**.

④ ▶ You see a preview of the image. Click the **OK** button.

End Task

Task 7: Changing the Colors Windows Uses

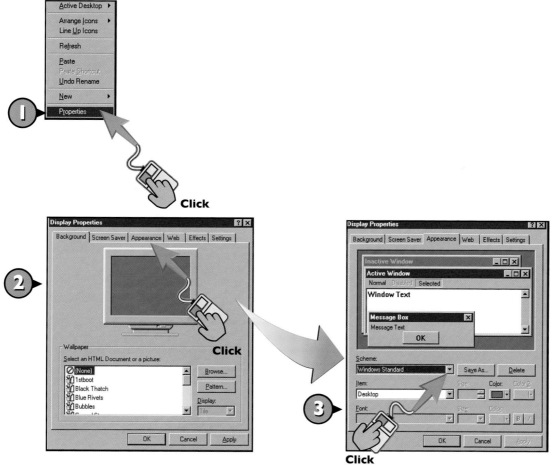

Windows enables you to change the sets of colors used for certain onscreen elements such as the title bar, background, and so on. These sets of colors are called *schemes*, and you can select colors that work best for you and your monitor. Lighter colors might, for example, make working in some Windows applications easier on your eyes. On the other hand, you might prefer bright and lively colors.

1. ► Right-click any blank area of the desktop, and then click **Properties**.

2. ► Click the **Appearance** tab.

3. ► From the **Scheme** drop-down list, select any of the available schemes.

✓ **Original Colors**
To revert to the original colors, click **Cancel** instead of **OK**. If you have already closed the dialog box, you can revert to the Windows Standard scheme by selecting it from the list.

Changing the Colors Windows Uses Continued

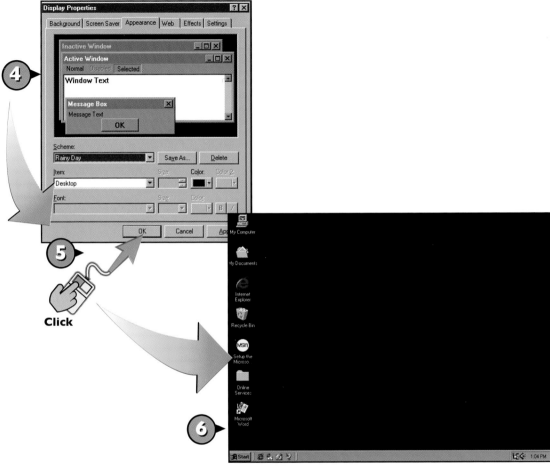

Click

④ The color scheme you selected (in this case, **Rainy Day**) appears in the sample box.

⑤ Click the **OK** button to accept the changes.

⑥ Windows uses the new set of colors you selected.

End Task

Task 8: Using Desktop Themes

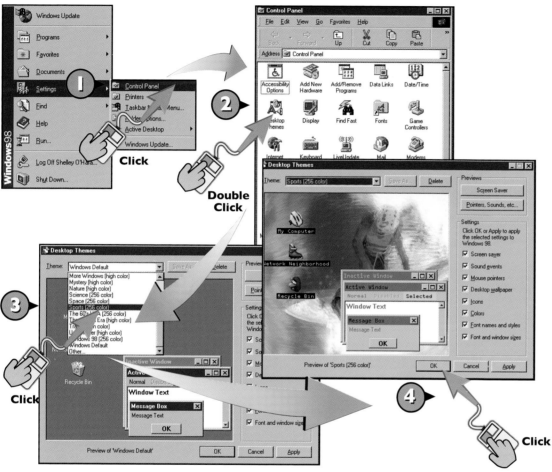

You can use a unified set of desktop, wallpaper, and mouse pointers, called a theme. Windows 98 comes with several child-related themes, which you can install and use.

✅ **Change Settings**
Check or uncheck any of the settings to select which features are included in the theme (screen saver, sounds, and so on).

✅ **Purchase More Themes**
You can purchase additional themes to use on your PC.

✅ **Install Themes**
To use the themes, they must be installed. If you don't see a **Themes** icon, the themes aren't installed. Install them (see "Installing Windows Components" in the next part).

1 ▶ Click the **Start** button, choose **Settings**, and select **Control Panel**.

2 ▶ Double-click the **Desktop Themes** icon.

3 ▶ Select a theme from the **Theme** drop-down list.

4 ▶ You see a preview of how the icons, the colors, and the desktop. If you like what you see, click **OK**; otherwise, select a different theme from the list.

End
Task

Page
121

Task 9: Using a Screen Saver

In the past, the concentration of bright or white colors on older monitors would, over time, burn into the screen. When this happened, you saw a "ghost" of the Windows screen on your display after you turned off your computer. A screen saver (a moving pattern of dark and light colors or images) helped protect your screen from burn-in by displaying a pattern whenever the computer was on but inactive. These days, screen savers are used mostly for fun.

 Preview the Screen Saver
If you want to see what the screen saver will look like when it is displayed on the full screen, click the **Preview** button to direct Windows to display the saver on the entire screen. Click the mouse button or press the spacebar to return to the **Display Properties** dialog box.

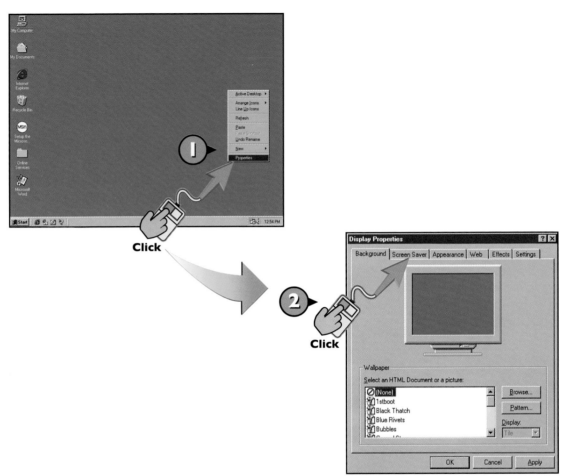

Click

Click

 Right-click any blank area of the desktop, and then click **Properties**.

Click the **Screen Saver** tab.

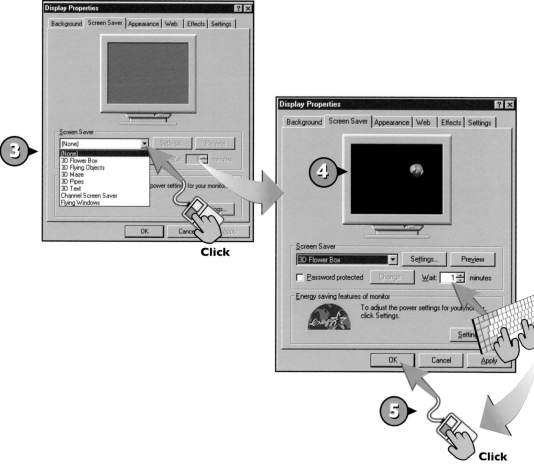

Click

Click

Screen Saver Options
Click the **Settings** button to select options for how the screen saver is displayed; these options vary depending on the screen saver. Make your choices and click the **OK** button.

Stop Screen Saver
When the screen saver is displayed, move the mouse or press the spacebar to return to the normal view.

Turn Off Screen Saver
To turn off the screen saver, invoke the **Display Properties** dialog box, click the **Screen Saver** tab, and select **None**. Click the **OK** button.

3 ▶ Click the **Screen Saver** drop-down list box arrow to display the list of available screen savers, and then select the screen saver you want to use.

4 ▶ The selected screen saver appears on the sample monitor. If you want to use it, type the number of minutes you want Windows to wait before it starts the screen saver in the **Wait** text box.

5 ▶ Click the **OK** button.

Task 10: Changing How Your Monitor Works

Start Here

Many monitors allow you to select certain options about how they operate—such as the number of colors they display or their resolution. (*Resolution* measures the number of pixels or picture elements displayed. An example of a common resolution is 800×600.) You might need to change your monitor's display properties if you get a new monitor, want to update your monitor driver, or want to change how the monitor looks.

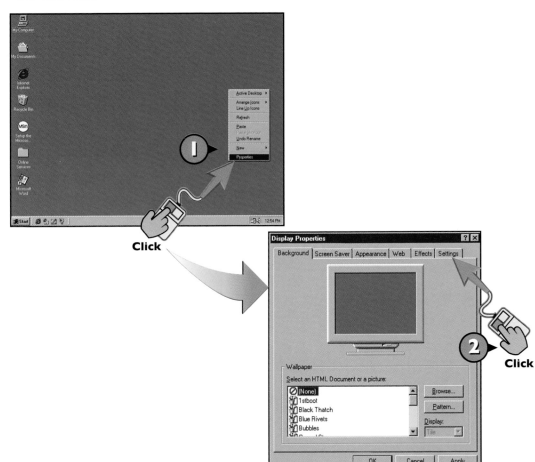

Click

Click

New Monitor?
To update a monitor or adapter, click the **Advanced** button on the **Settings** tab, and then select either the **Adapter** or **Monitor** tab. Click the **Change** button and follow the wizard's instructions for installing a new monitor or adapter.

Right-click any blank area of the desktop, and then click **Properties**.

2 ▶ Click the **Settings** tab.

Next Step

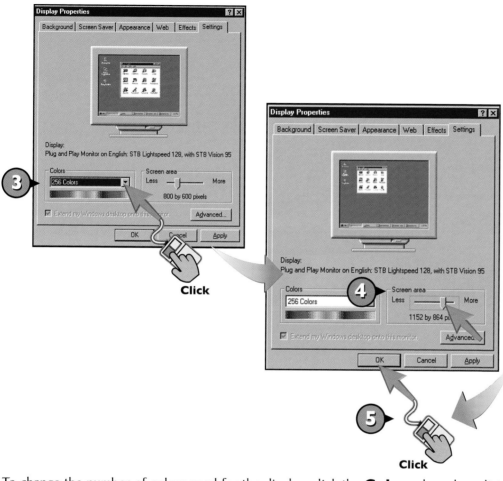

Click

Click

3 To change the number of colors used for the display, click the **Colors** drop-down list and choose the number you want.

4 To change the resolution, drag the **Screen area** bar to the desired setting.

5 Click the **OK** button.

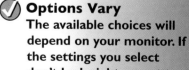

Options Vary
The available choices will depend on your monitor. If the settings you select don't look right, revert to the original ones.

End Task

Task 11: Changing How the Desktop Icons Look

Another way to experiment with the appearance of the desktop is to change how the icons are displayed. You can select a different picture for any of the default icons. Windows 98 comes with several icons to choose from. You can also select the size and colors used for icons on the desktop.

Start Here

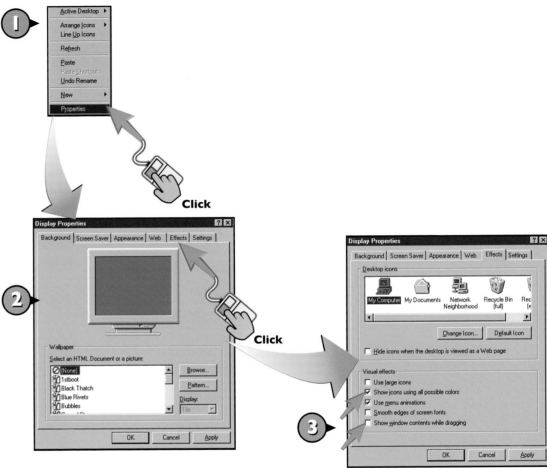

Click

Click

✓ **Original Icons**
To go back to the original icon, display the **Effects** tab and select the icon. Click the **Default Icon** button, and then click the **OK** button.

1 ▶ Right-click any blank area of the desktop, and then click **Properties**.

2 ▶ Click the **Effects** tab.

3 ▶ Select the visual effects you want in the **Visual effects** section. A check mark next to an option indicates that the option is active. If an option is unchecked, it is inactive.

Next Step

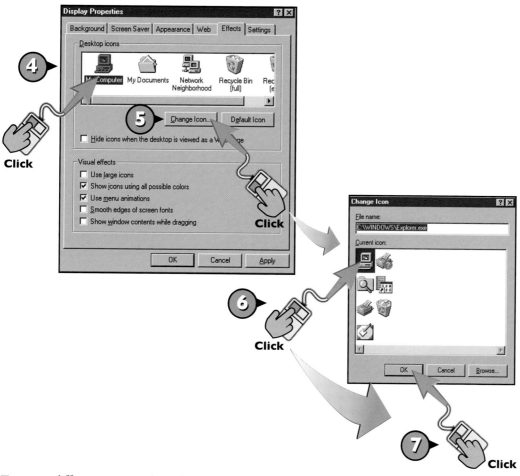

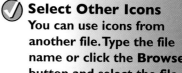

4 ▶ To use a different icon, select the icon you want to change.

5 ▶ Click the **Change Icon** button.

6 ▶ Select the icon you want to use instead.

7 ▶ Click the **OK** button in the **Change Icon** dialog box, and then close the **OK** button in the **Display Properties** dialog box.

✅ Select Other Icons
You can use icons from another file. Type the file name or click the **Browse** button and select the file to use.

Task 12: Viewing the Desktop as a Web Page

If you have used the Internet, you might be comfortable with the methods used on it for viewing content. For example, when you browse the Internet, you can click a link to display its contents. You can set up your desktop to browse its contents just like a Web page. You also can display Web channels, which you can use to browse the Internet. (For more information about browsing the Internet, see Part 9, "Connecting to Online Services and the Internet.")

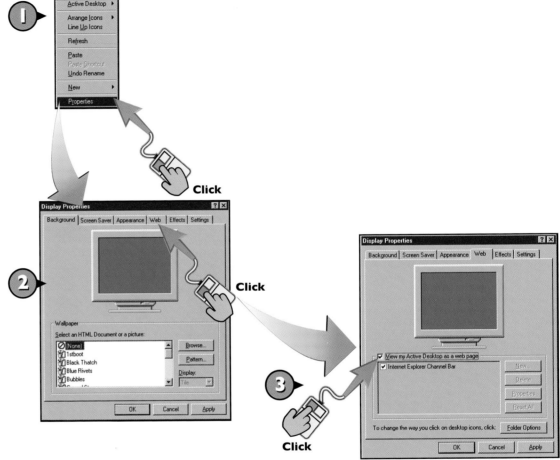

Click

Click

Click

✓ **Back to Regular Desktop**
To revert to the regular desktop, right-click a blank area of the desktop, choose **Active Desktop**, and click **View As Web Page** to deselect this option.

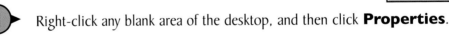

1 Right-click any blank area of the desktop, and then click **Properties**.

2 Click the **Web** tab.

3 Check the **View my Active Desktop as a web page** check box.

Next Step

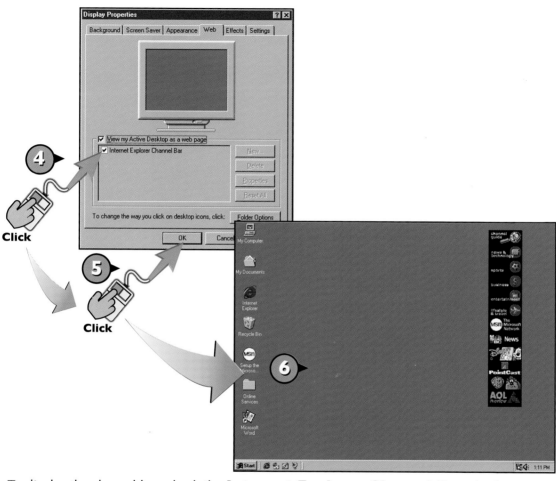

Browsing Folders
You can use the Folder Options to set up how folders are displayed. Refer to Part 3, "Working with Disks, Folders, and Files," for more information about working with folders in Web view.

Try This Method
You can also click the **Start** button, select the **Settings** option, click **Active Desktop**, and select **View as Web Page** to turn on Web view.

4 ▶ To display the channel bar, check the **Internet Explorer Channel Bar** check box.

5 ▶ Click the **OK** button.

6 ▶ The desktop is displayed as a Web page.

Task 13: Working with Channels

You can display your desktop as a Web page to make your system easy to browse, and to make channels available. *Channels are sites designed specifically for Internet Explorer. You can have content from channels delivered right to your desktop. (For more information about browsing the Internet and channels, see Part 9.)*

✓ Subscribe to Channel
You can subscribe to channels and have the content downloaded according to the schedule you specify. You can also add channels to your channel bar. For more information, consult online help or Part 9.

✓ Hide Channel
To hide the channel bar, right-click a blank area of the desktop, choose **Active Desktop**, and click **View As Web Page** to deselect it.

✓ First Time?
If you have not yet viewed the content, you will see a link. Click it to connect to your Internet provider and download the content.

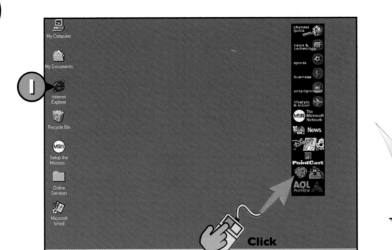

Start Here

Click

 To view a channel, click it.

2 Windows opens a full view of the channel window and displays the content if that content has been downloaded or viewed before.

End Task

Task 14: Changing the System Date and Time

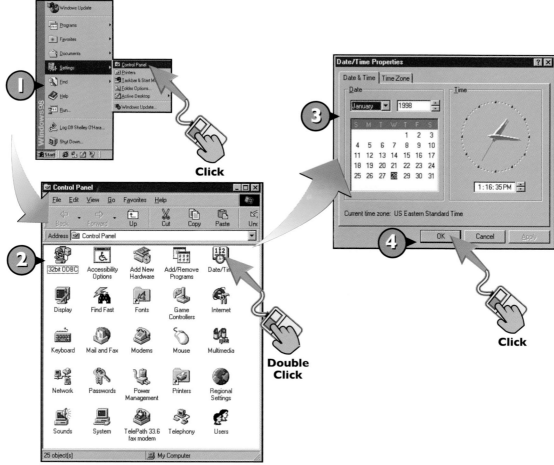

Start Here

Click

Double Click

Click

You can place the pointer over the time in the taskbar to display the current date. If your system clock is wrong, you should correct it because Windows stamps the time and date on every file you save.

✓ **Shortcut**
Display the **Date/Time Properties** dialog box by double-clicking the time in the taskbar.

✓ **Dead Battery**
If the date is wrong, it could indicate that you have a dead battery.

✓ **Making a Change**
If the month is wrong, display the **Month** drop-down list and select the correct month. If the year is incorrect, type the correct one in the appropriate text box or use the up and down arrows to adjust it. If the date is wrong, click the correct date on the calendar. Use the up and down arrows to adjust the time.

1 ▶ Click the **Start** menu, click **Settings**, and select **Control Panel**.

2 ▶ Double-click the **Date/Time** icon.

3 ▶ Correct the date and time.

4 ▶ Click the **OK** button.

End Task

Task 15: Changing How the Mouse Works

You can adjust the mouse buttons and double-click speed to make using the mouse more comfortable for you. Suppose, for example, that you are left-handed; switching the left and right mouse buttons can make your work much easier. Likewise, if you are having trouble getting the double-click right, you can change the double-click speed on the mouse. You can also slow your pointer speed down so that you can easily find your mouse onscreen when you move it quickly.

 Go Back to First Settings
Follow the same procedure if you make a change and want to revert to the original settings.

 Test Double-Clicking
You can test the double-click speed by double-clicking in the **Test** box. When you double-click correctly, a Jack-in-the-box pops out. Double-click again, and Jack goes back into the box.

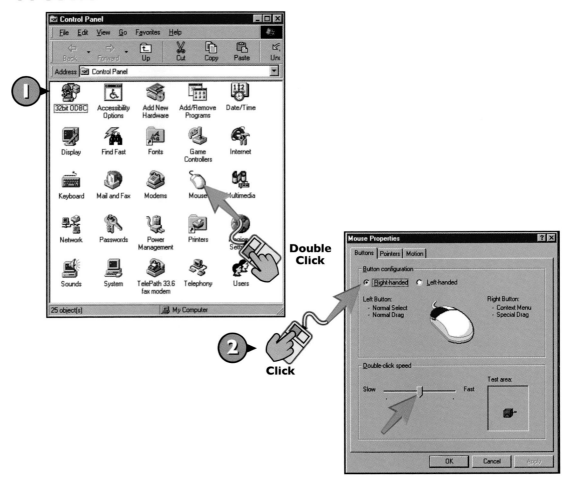

Double Click

Click

1. Double-click the **Mouse** icon in the **Control Panel** (refer to Task 12 if you need help opening the **Control Panel**).

2. If you want to switch the mouse buttons, select the **Left-handed** radio button. To change the double-click speed, drag the **Double-click speed** lever between **Slow** and **Fast**.

Next Step

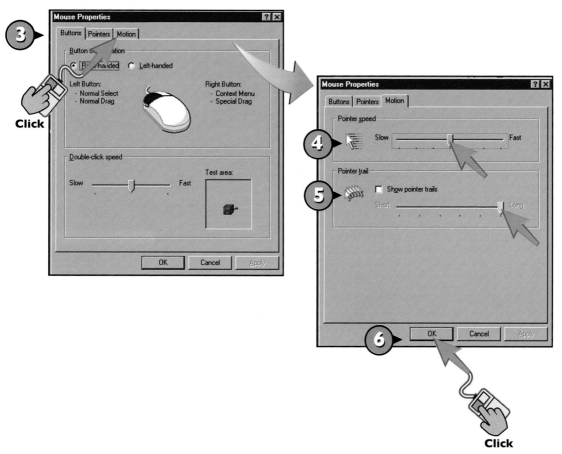

Click

Click

Click the **Motion** tab to change the pointer speed or to leave a mouse trail.

Adjust the pointer speed by dragging the **Pointer speed** lever between **Slow** and **Fast**.

To show a pointer trail, check the **Show pointer trails** option, and then select the length of the trail by dragging the **Pointer trail** lever between **Short** and **Long**.

Click the **OK** button.

Pointers?
See the next task for information on changing the look of the mouse pointers.

Task 16: Changing How the Mouse Pointers Look

You can change the way the mouse pointer appears onscreen. Depending on the action, the pointer takes several different shapes. For instance, when Windows is busy, you see an hourglass. You can select a different set of shapes (called a *scheme*) if you prefer.

Start Here

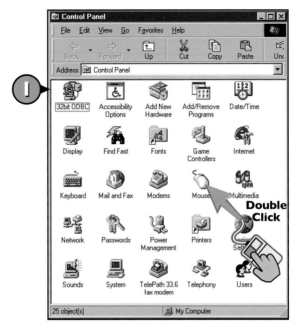

Double Click

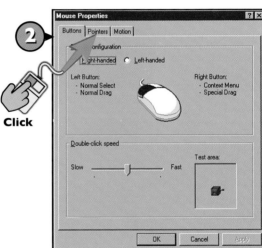

Click

✅ **Back to Original Pointers**

To go back to the default scheme, display the **Pointers** tab of the **Mouse Properties** dialog box, and then select **None** from the **Scheme** drop-down list.

 Double-click the **Mouse** icon in the **Control Panel** (refer to Task 12 if you need help opening the **Control Panel**).

 Click the **Pointers** tab.

Next Step

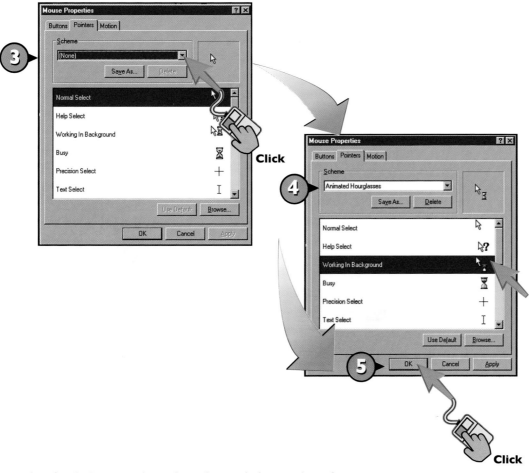

Click

Click

3 ▶ Display the **Scheme** drop-down list and choose the scheme you want to use.

4 ▶ A preview of each pointer in the chosen scheme (in this case, **Animated Hourglasses**) is displayed.

5 ▶ Click **OK** to accept the changes and to close the dialog box.

✓ **Single Changes**
You can select which pointer to use for each individual action. Simply select the action you want to change, click the **Browse** button, select the pointer you want to use, and click **Open**. Do this for each action you want to change, and then click the **OK** button.

End Task

Task 17: Playing Sounds for Certain Windows Actions

When you perform certain actions in Windows 98, you might hear a sound. For instance, you hear a sound when Windows 98 is started. You might hear a sound when an alert box is displayed. You can stick with the default sounds, or you can select a different sound to use for each key Windows event.

Double Click

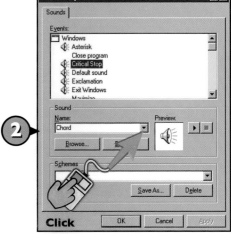

Click

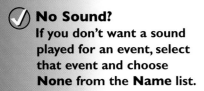

No Sound?
If you don't want a sound played for an event, select that event and choose **None** from the **Name** list.

Select a Scheme
If you have sound schemes, you can select a set of sounds by displaying the **Schemes** drop-down list in the **Sound Properties** dialog box. Select the scheme you want and then click **OK**.

 Double-click the **Sounds** icon in the **Control Panel** (refer to Task 12 if you need help opening the **Control Panel**).

 Select the sound event you want to change, and then display the **Name** drop-down list to select the sound that you want to assign.

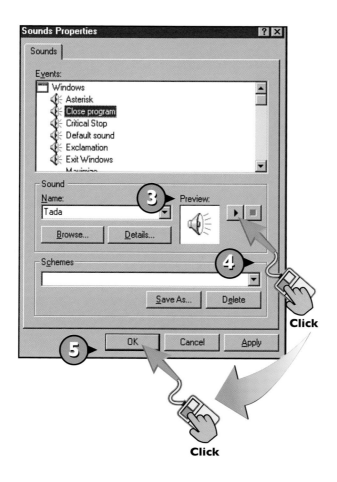

Sounds Properties

Sounds

Events:

Windows
　Asterisk
　Close program
　Critical Stop
　Default sound
　Exclamation
　Exit Windows
　Maximize

Sound

Name:
Tada

Browse...　Details...

Preview:

Schemes

Save As...　Delete

Click

OK　Cancel　Apply

5

3

4

Click

4 A preview icon becomes visible, and the **Play** button is activated.

5 To hear a preview of the sound, click the **Play** button.

6 Click **OK** to accept the changes and to close the dialog box.

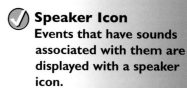 **Speaker Icon**
Events that have sounds
associated with them are
displayed with a speaker
icon.

End
Task

Task 18: Setting Up Windows for Multiple Users

If more than one person uses your PC, you might want to personalize certain Windows settings for each person. For instance, you can customize the desktop, **Start** menu, **Favorites** folder, Web page subscriptions, **My Documents** folder, and more. Each person can set up Windows the way he or she wants and then create a user profile. Each time that person logs on, all those settings will be used.

Start Here

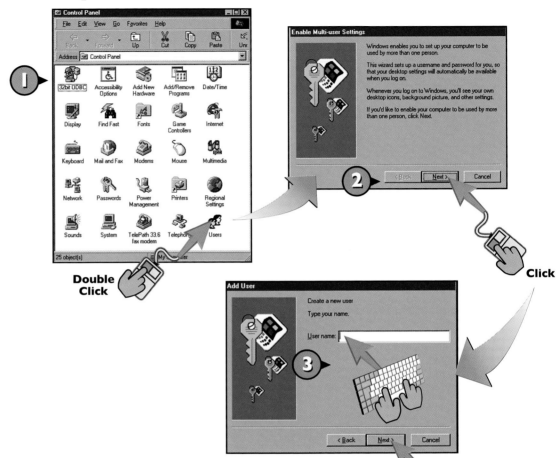

Double Click

Click

1 ▶ Double-click the **Users** icon in the **Control Panel** to start the **Multiple Users** wizard. If you need help opening the **Control Panel**, refer to Task 12.

2 ▶ Click the **Next** button.

3 ▶ Type the name of the person you are setting up, and then click **Next**.

Next Step

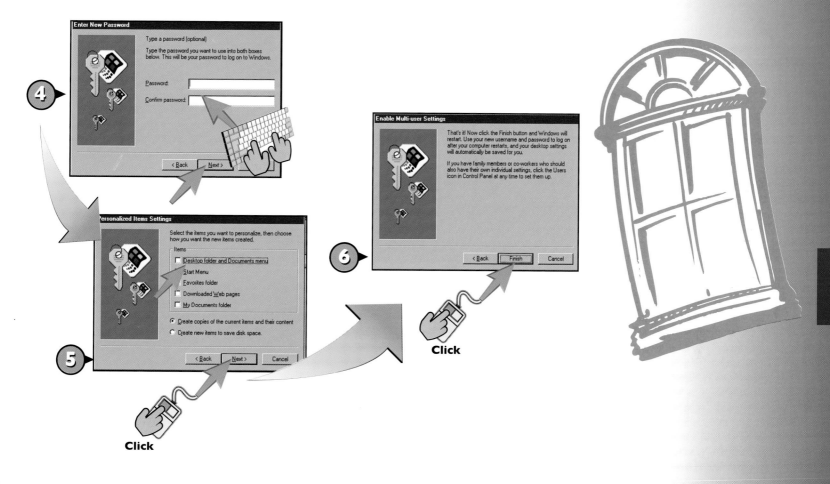

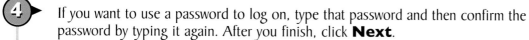

Click

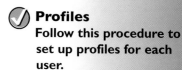

Click

4 If you want to use a password to log on, type that password and then confirm the password by typing it again. After you finish, click **Next**.

5 From the **Items** section, select the items you want to save in this profile. After you finish, click **Next**.

6 Click the **Finish** button. Windows will be restarted, and you will be prompted to type your user name and password in order to log on.

✔ Profiles
Follow this procedure to set up profiles for each user.

You can employ certain features of Windows 98 to make it easier to use. You can select different settings for the keyboard, sounds, display, and mouse.

Task 19: Setting Up Windows for the Impaired

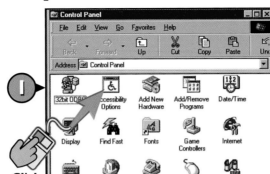

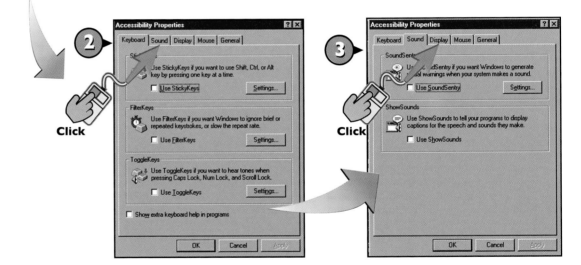

Click

Click

Click

✓ **Cancel Changes**
Any changes you make in this dialog box can easily be reversed. Simply choose **Cancel** to close the dialog box.

✓ **Key Options**
You can use StickyKeys to press one key at a time for key combinations. Use FilterKeys to ignore brief repeated keystrokes. Use ToggleKeys to play a tone when you have pressed Caps Lock, Num Lock, or Scroll Lock.

1 Double-click the **Accessibility Options** icon in the **Control Panel**. If you need help reaching the **Control Panel**, refer to Task 12.

2 Enable any keyboard features by checking the appropriate check box. After you finish, click the **Sound** tab.

3 Select to display visual warnings and/or captions for alert messages, and then click the **Display** tab.

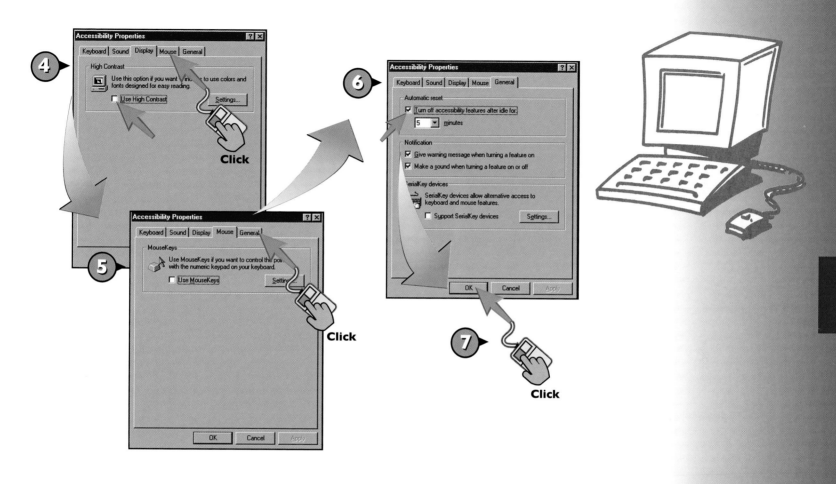

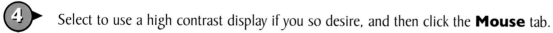

4 Select to use a high contrast display if you so desire, and then click the **Mouse** tab.

5 Select to use the numeric keypad to control the mouse, and then click the **General** tab.

6 Make changes as needed to the reset and notification options.

7 Click the **OK** button.

✔ **Not Sure About an Option?**
If you aren't sure what an option does, right-click and select What's This to see a pop-up explanation.

Task 20: Controlling Power Settings

If you do not use your computer for a period of time, you can select to save energy by using the power-management features. You can put the computer on standby, turn off the monitor, and turn off the hard disk after a set interval of inactivity.

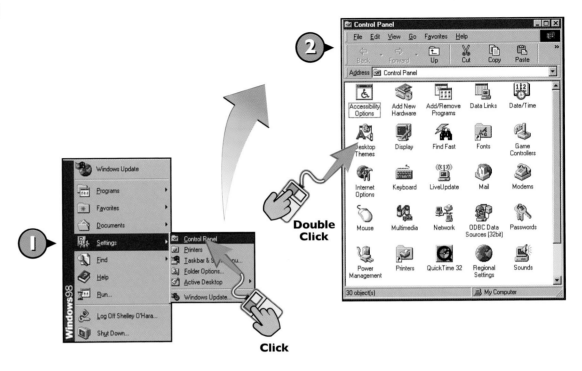

Double Click

Click

✓ **Use a Scheme**
You can also select from several power schemes. Display the **Power schemes** drop-down list and select the scheme you want.

1 ▸ Click the **Start** button, choose **Settings**, and select **Control Panel**.

2 ▸ Double-click the **Power Management** icon.

Next Step

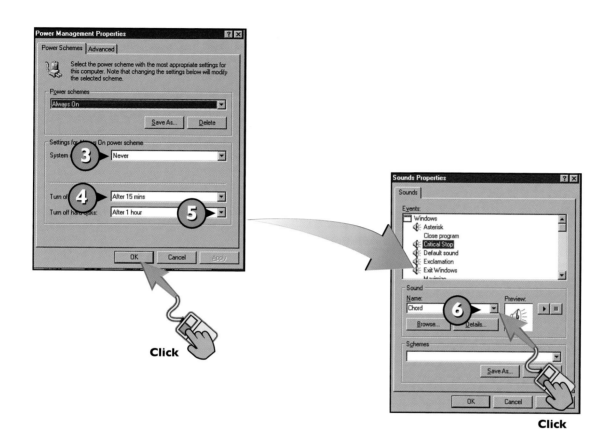

Click

Click

3 Select when to use system standby.

4 Select when to turn off the monitor.

5 Select when to turn off the hard disk.

6 Click **OK**.

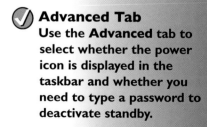

Advanced Tab
Use the **Advanced** tab to select whether the power icon is displayed in the taskbar and whether you need to type a password to deactivate standby.

End Task

PART 6

Setting Up Programs

Most of the time you spend using your computer will be spent using some application. To make it as easy as possible, Windows 98 enables you to set up several ways for starting programs. You can create shortcuts to a program and place the shortcut on the desktop to make it more accessible. You can rearrange the programs on the Start menu so that they are more suited to how you work. You can install new programs and remove programs you no longer use. This part shows you how to accomplish all of these setup tasks and more.

Tasks

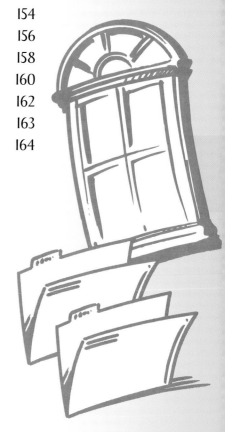

Task 1: Adding Shortcuts

You can create shortcuts and place them on the desktop to provide quick access to programs. You then double-click a shortcut to quickly start that program—without having to open menus and folders.

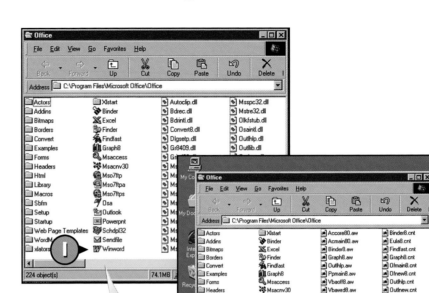

Drag

Drop

✓ Shortcut to Files or Folders

You can create shortcut icons to files or folders (covered in Part 3, "Working with Disks, Folders, and Files") or to your printer (covered in Part 4, "Printing with Windows").

✓ Can't Find File?

If you can't find the program file, try searching for it. Finding a particular file is covered in Part 3.

 In either **My Computer** or **Windows Explorer** (in this case, **My Computer**), display the program file for which you want to create a shortcut icon.

 Holding down your right mouse button, drag the program file from the window to your desktop.

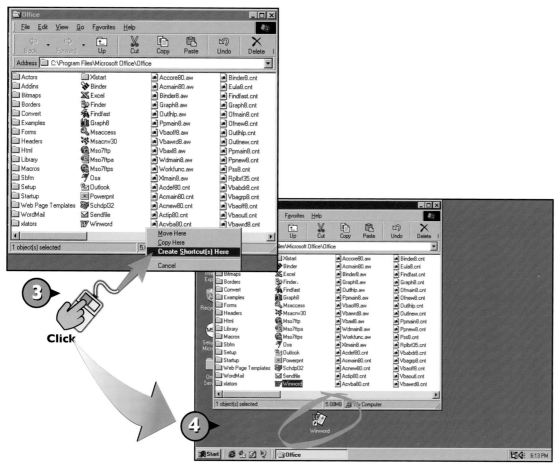

3 Release the button, and then choose **Create Shortcut(s) Here** from the ensuing shortcut menu.

4 Windows adds the shortcut to your desktop.

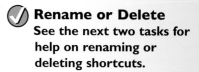

✓ **Rename or Delete**
See the next two tasks for help on renaming or deleting shortcuts.

Task 2: Renaming Shortcuts

When you create a shortcut, Windows 98 assigns a name to the icon, but you might want to use a different name. For instance, rather than the name **Winword**, you might prefer **Word**. You can rename any of the shortcut icons on your desktop.

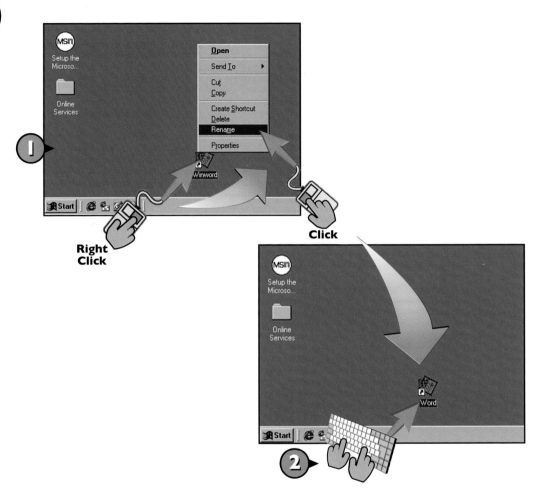

1 Right-click the selected icon, and then click the **Rename** command.

2 Type the new shortcut name, and press **Enter**.

Task 3: Deleting Shortcuts

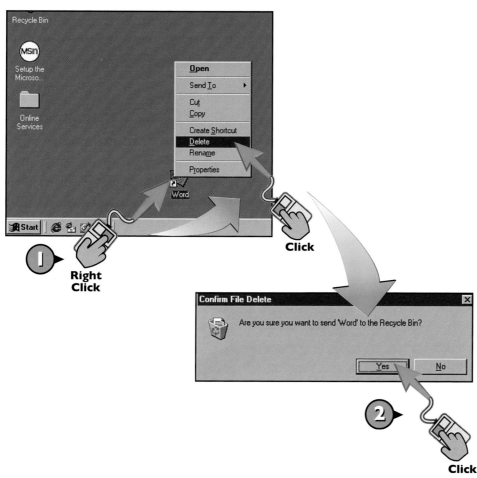

As time passes, your needs for programs might change, and the desktop might become cluttered with program icons you no longer need. Just as you can create new shortcuts as you add new programs, you can delete shortcuts you no longer use.

Program Not Deleted
Deleting a shortcut does not delete that program from your hard drive. To delete the program, you must uninstall it or delete the program and its related folders and files.

Restore Shortcut
If you change your mind about deleting an item, you can restore items you've relegated to the **Recycle Bin**. To do so, double-click the **Recycle Bin**. In the **Recycle Bin** window, right-click the item you want to restore and choose **Restore**. The item returns to its original location. Close the **Recycle Bin** by clicking the **Close** button.

 Right-click the selected icon, and click the **Delete** command.

 In the **Confirm File Delete** dialog box, click **Yes** to delete the shortcut.

Task 4: Adding Programs to the Start Menu

When you install most programs, they are added automatically to the **Start** menu. If a program is not added during installation, you can add it yourself.

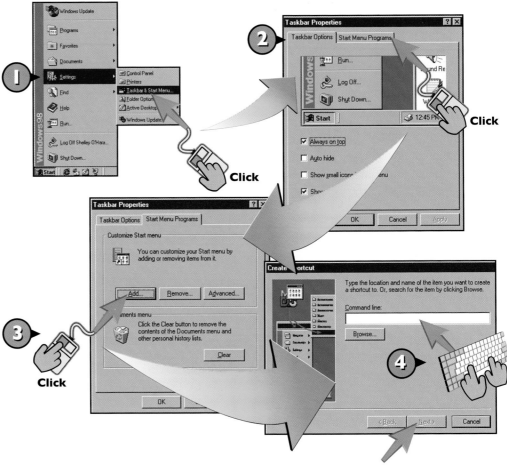

Click

Click

Click

Click

✓ **Browse for Program**
If you don't know the command line, click the **Browse** button, and then select the folder and the program name from the **Browse** dialog box.

① Click **Start**, select the **Settings** command, and then click **Taskbar & Start Menu**.

② Click the **Start Menu Programs** tab.

③ Click the **Add** button.

④ Enter the command line for the program you want to add, and then click the **Next** button.

Next Step

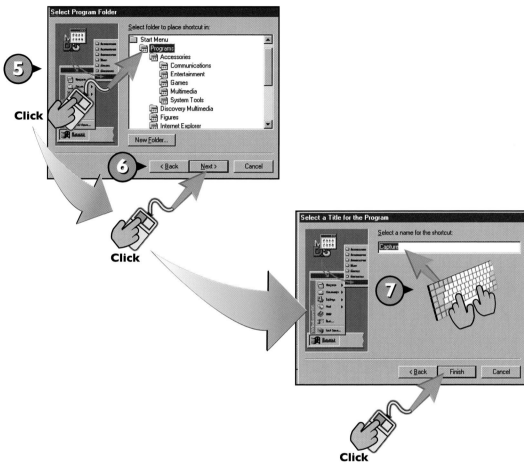

Click

Click

Click

5 ▶ Select the folder in which you want to place the program.

6 ▶ Click the **Next** button.

7 ▶ Enter a name in the text box or accept the one Windows displays. Click the **Finish** button to add the new program.

✓ **New Folder**
You can click the **New Folder** button to add a new folder (also see the task titled "Adding Folders to the Start Menu" later in this part).

✓ **Remove a Program**
To remove a program from the **Start** menu, see the next task.

End Task

Task 5: Deleting Programs from the Start Menu

If your **Start** menu becomes cluttered, you might want to delete icons for programs that you don't use. At first, you might go a little crazy and add all kinds of icons. But after you use the computer more and more, you might want to streamline the **Start** menu and weed out programs that you don't use.

✓ Remove a Folder

You can follow this procedure to remove a folder from the **Start** menu. Simply select the folder and then click the **Remove** button. You are prompted to confirm the removal; click **Yes**. The folder and all its contents are removed.

✓ Program Files Not Deleted

Keep in mind that removing a program from the **Start** menu does not remove the program and its files from your hard disk. To do this, you must uninstall the program or manually delete it and its related folders and files. See Task 10, "Uninstalling Applications."

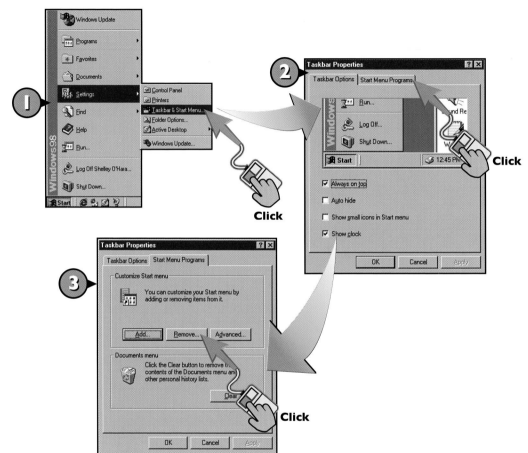

Click

Click

Click

1. Click **Start**, select the **Settings** command, and then click the **Taskbar & Start Menu** command.

2. Click the **Start Menu Programs** tab.

3. Click the **Remove** button.

Next Step

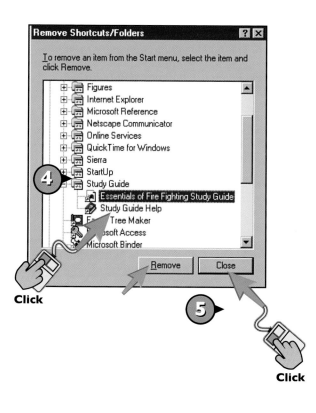

Remove Shortcuts/Folders

To remove an item from the Start menu, select the item and click Remove.

- ⊞ Figures
- ⊞ Internet Explorer
- ⊞ Microsoft Reference
- ⊞ Netscape Communicator
- ⊞ Online Services
- ⊞ QuickTime for Windows
- ⊞ Sierra
- ⊞ StartUp
- ⊟ Study Guide
  - Essentials of Fire Fighting Study Guide
  - Study Guide Help
- Tree Maker
- Microsoft Access
- Microsoft Binder

4

[Remove] [Close]

Click

5

Click

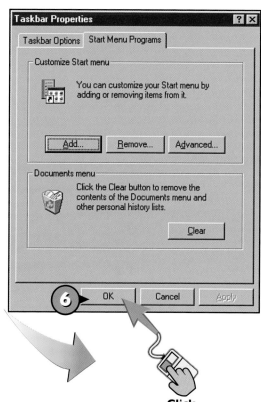

Taskbar Properties

Taskbar Options | **Start Menu Programs**

Customize Start menu

You can customize your Start menu by adding or removing items from it.

[Add...] [Remove...] [Advanced...]

Documents menu

Click the Clear button to remove the contents of the Documents menu and other personal history lists.

[Clear]

6 [OK] [Cancel] [Apply]

Click

4 ▶ Select the program you want to remove, and then click the **Remove** button.

5 ▶ Click the **Close** button to close this dialog box.

6 ▶ Click **OK** to close the **Taskbar Properties** dialog box.

✓ **Expand Folder**
In order to display and select the program you want to remove, you might need to expand the folder listings. Click the plus sign next to the folder that contains the desired program.

End Task

Task 6: Adding Folders to the Start Menu

When you install a new program, that program's installation sets up program folders and icons for itself. If you don't like the arrangement of the folders and icons, you can change it. For instance, if more than one person uses your PC, you might set up folders for each person and then add the programs that a certain person uses to his or her folder.

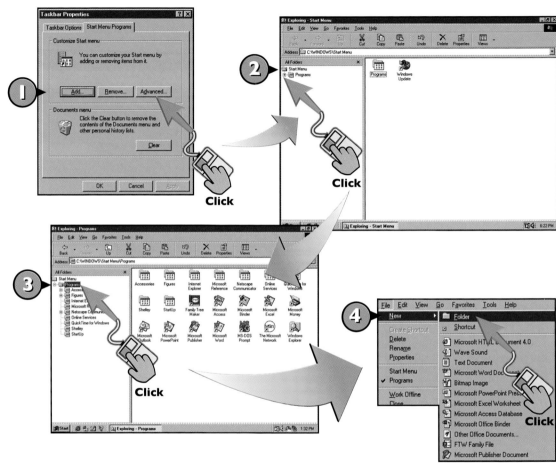

 Display Menu
To display the **Start Menu Programs** tab, click **Start**, **Settings** and **Taskbar & Start Menu**. Then click the tab.

 Delete a Folder
You can delete folders. To do so, simply right-click the folder and select the **Delete** command from the shortcut menu. Click **Yes** to confirm the deletion.

1 ▶ Click the **Advanced** button in the **Start Menu Programs** tab. Refer to the last task if you need help reaching this tab.

2 ▶ The **Start** menu is displayed in **Windows Explorer**. If needed, click the plus button next to the **Programs** entry to expand the list.

3 ▶ Select the folder in which the new folder should be placed. For this example, I'm placing the new folder within the **Programs** folder, so I've clicked **Programs**.

4 ▶ Click **File**, select **New**, and then click **Folder**.

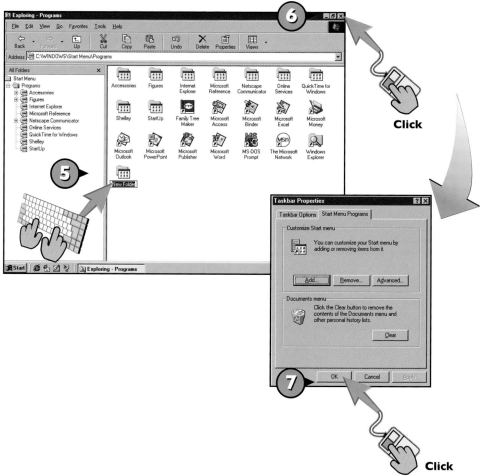

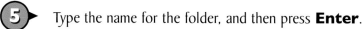

5 Type the name for the folder, and then press **Enter**.

6 Click the **Close** button.

7 Click the **OK** button in the **Taskbar Properties** dialog box.

Use Windows Explorer
If you follow the steps in this task, you'll see the **Programs** folder in a **Windows Explorer** window. You can use any of the commands and features of Windows Explorer to work with the contents of your **Programs** folder.

End Task

Task 7: Rearranging the Start Menu

After you set up folders, you can organize your **Start** menu, putting the program icons in the folder and order you want.

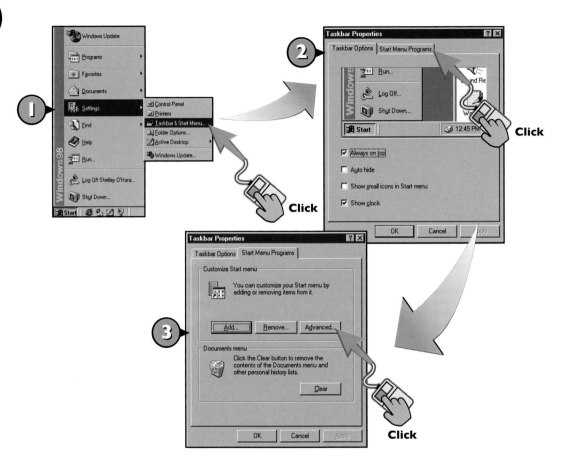

Click

Click

Click

✅ **Drag to Move**
You can drag an existing program to a new location. Simply click the program name and then drag it to the new location on the **Start** menu.

1 ▶ Click **Start**, select the **Settings** command, and then click the **Taskbar & Start Menu** command.

2 ▶ Click the **Start Menu Programs** tab.

3 ▶ Click the **Advanced** button.

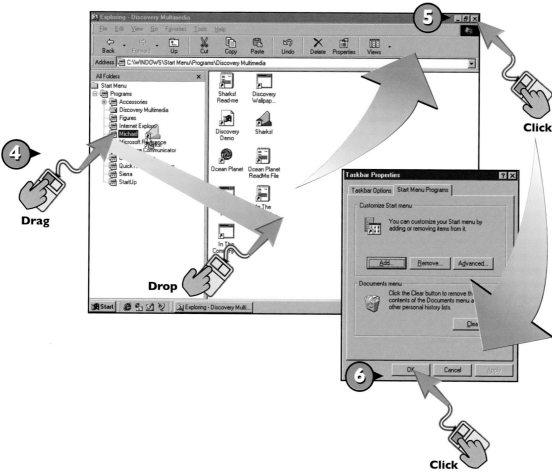

Click

Drag

Drop

Click

Click

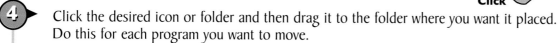

④▸ Click the desired icon or folder and then drag it to the folder where you want it placed. Do this for each program you want to move.

⑤▸ Click the **Close** button.

⑥▸ Click the **OK** button in the **Taskbar Properties** dialog box.

Task 8: Starting an Application When You Start Windows

Windows enables you to start one or more programs at the same time that you start Windows. Applications you might want to open automatically include those that you use every day or first thing every morning.

✓ Starts Only When Windows Starts

If you don't turn off your computer each night and then turn it on again when you begin work, these programs will not be started each morning. They are started only when you start Windows.

✓ Remove Program

To remove an icon from the **StartUp** window, click the **Remove** button in the **Start Menu Programs** tab of the **Taskbar Properties** dialog box to display the **Remove Shortcuts/Folders** dialog box. Then choose the item you want to remove from the menu and click the **Remove** button. Close the **Remove Shortcuts/ Folders** dialog box, and then click **OK**.

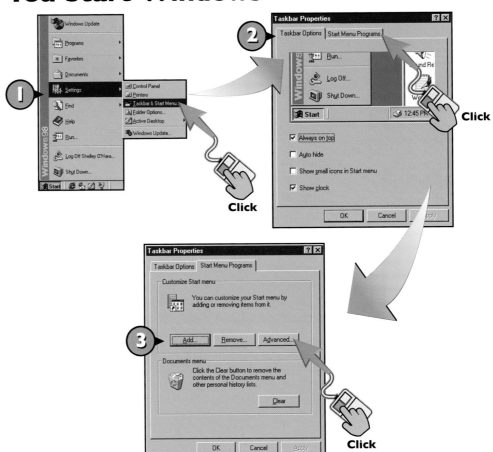

Click

Click

Click

I ▶ Click **Start**, select the **Settings** command, and then click the **Taskbar & Start Menu** command.

2 ▶ Click the **Start Menu Programs** tab.

3 ▶ Click the **Advanced** button.

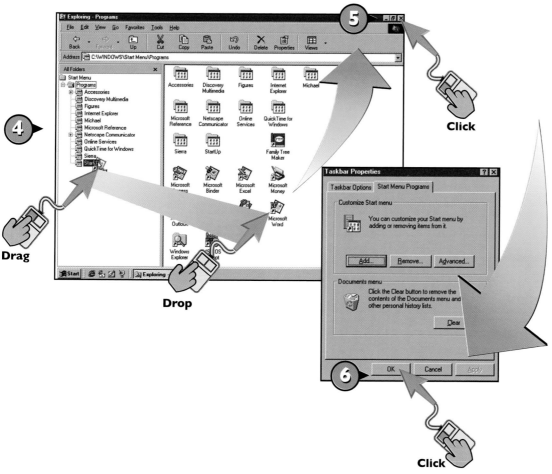

Click

Drag

Drop

Click

4 Select the icon for the program that you want to add to your **Startup** folder (in this case, Microsoft Word). Hold down the **Ctrl** key and drag the icon to the **StartUp** folder.

5 Click the **Close** button.

6 Click the **OK** button in the **Taskbar Properties** dialog box.

✓ Expand the List
If necessary, expand the **Programs** list to display the **StartUp** folder.

End Task

Task 9: Installing Applications

When you bought your computer, it might have come with certain programs already installed. If you want to add to these, you can purchase additional programs and then add them to your system. Installing a new program basically copies the program files to a folder on your system and then adds a program icon for starting that program. The program's installation might also make changes to other files or programs on your system.

✓ **Use the Run Command**
If this procedure does not work, you can use the **Run** command to run the installation program. Insert the **CD-ROM** or disk into the appropriate drive, and then click the **Start** button and choose **Run**. Enter the disk drive and command for the installation program and click **OK**. Follow the onscreen instructions.

Click

Double Click

Click

1 Click **Start**, select **Settings**, and click **Control Panel**.

2 Double-click the **Add/Remove Programs** icon.

3 Click the **Install** button.

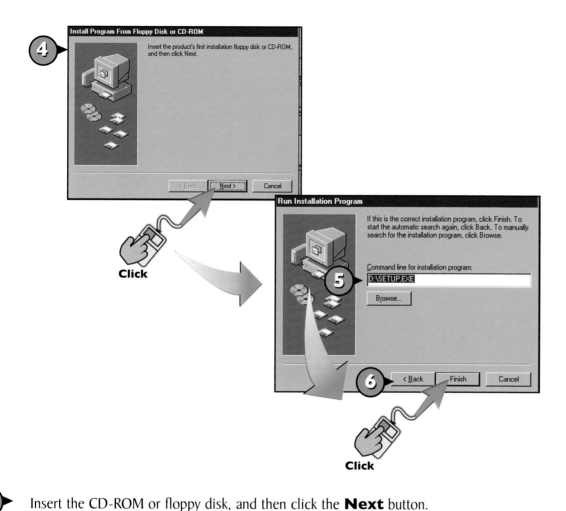

Install Program From Floppy Disk or CD-ROM

Insert the product's first installation floppy disk or CD-ROM, and then click Next.

< Back   Next >   Cancel

Click

Run Installation Program

If this is the correct installation program, click Finish. To start the automatic search again, click Back. To manually search for the installation program, click Browse.

Command line for installation program:
D:\SETUP.EXE

Browse...

< Back   Finish   Cancel

Click

4 ▶ Insert the CD-ROM or floppy disk, and then click the **Next** button.

5 ▶ Windows looks on both the floppy disk and the CD-ROM for an installation program. When it finds this file, it displays it in the **Run Installation Program** dialog box.

6 ▶ Click the **Finish** button, and then follow the onscreen instructions for your particular program.

✓ **Uninstall a Program**
For help on uninstalling applications, see the next task.

✓ **Start Menu Icon**
The installation program usually adds an icon to your **Start** menu so that you can easily start the program. If it does not, you can add one for the program. Refer to Task 4, "Adding Programs to the Start Menu."

End Task

Task 10: Uninstalling Applications

You can remove a shortcut icon or an item from the **Start** menu, but doing so leaves that program on your hard disk. When you want to get rid of the program and its files entirely, you can uninstall it. You should move any data files from your program folders if, for example, you plan to use them in another program.

✓ Not Listed?

Some programs can't be uninstalled via the **Install/Uninstall** tab. If your program is not listed, you must use a different procedure. Check your program documentation for specific instructions.

✓ Special Uninstall Programs

You can purchase programs to keep track of what programs you have installed, where they are, and what changes they have made to your system. You can use such a program to uninstall programs not listed in the Windows **Install/Uninstall** tab.

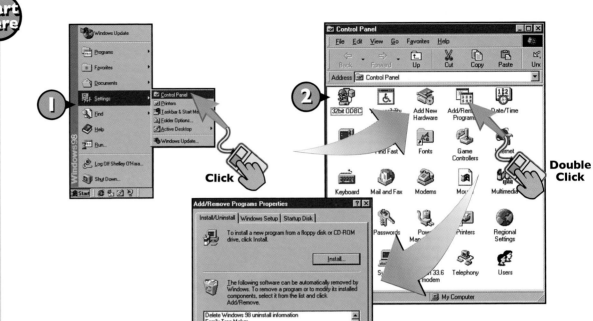

Click

Double Click

Click

Click

1. Click **Start**, select **Settings**, and click **Control Panel**.

2. Double-click the **Add/Remove Programs** icon.

3. Click the program you want to remove.

4. Click the **Add/Remove** button. The program is removed.

Task 11: Using the MS-DOS Prompt

Start Here

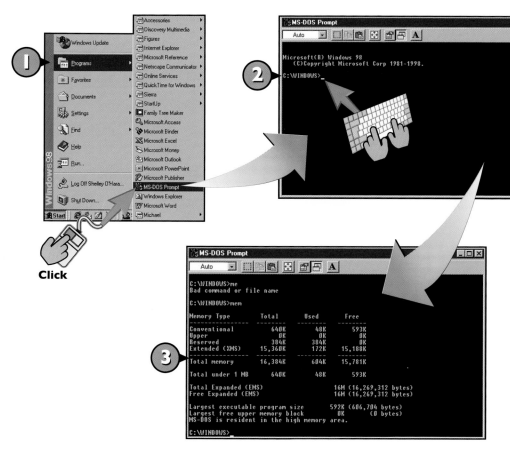

Click

Sometimes you'll want to access the **DOS** prompt from Windows. For example, you might want to run a **DOS** application or use **DOS** commands. You can run any program by typing the appropriate **DOS** command. Windows provides a **DOS** prompt window that you can open while working in Windows.

✔ **Will Mouse Work?**
Your mouse will work in the **DOS Prompt** window only if you have loaded a mouse driver to **DOS**. For instructions on doing this, refer to your mouse documentation.

✔ **Enlarge Window**
Press **Alt+Enter** to enlarge the DOS window to full screen. Press **Alt+Enter** again to restore the DOS window to its original size.

✔ **Exit DOS Prompt**
When you are finished working in DOS, type **exit** and press **Enter** to close the **MS-DOS Prompt** window.

1️⃣ Click **Start**, select **Programs**, and click **MS-DOS Prompt**.

2️⃣ Type the desired command and press **Enter**.

3️⃣ You can see the results of the command you typed.

End Task

Task 12: Installing Windows Components

If you have a new PC, it probably came with Windows already installed. As a result, you might not know which components are installed and which are not. Likewise, if you have upgraded to Windows 98, you might not have installed all the components when you performed the installation. If you want to add components or simply to view what else might be available, you can do so.

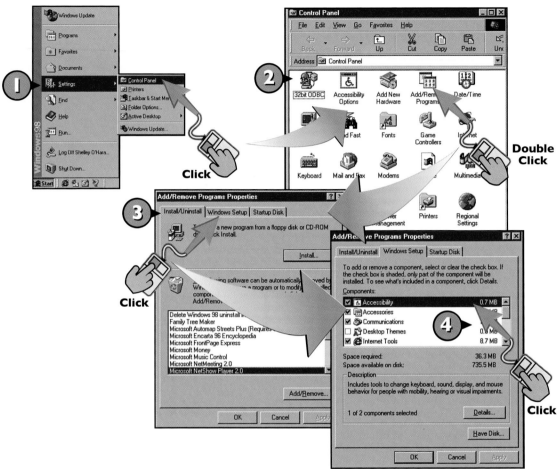

Click

Double Click

Click

Click

Click

✓ **Upgrading Windows**
For information on upgrading Windows, see Part 8, "Maintaining Your System."

✓ **Checks Mean?**
If an item is checked, it is installed. Items that are gray and checked have some of the items installed.

1 ▶ Click **Start**, select **Settings**, and click **Control Panel**.

2 ▶ Double-click the **Add/Remove Programs** icon.

3 ▶ Click the **Windows Setup** tab.

4 ▶ Select the feature you want to change or check.

Next Step

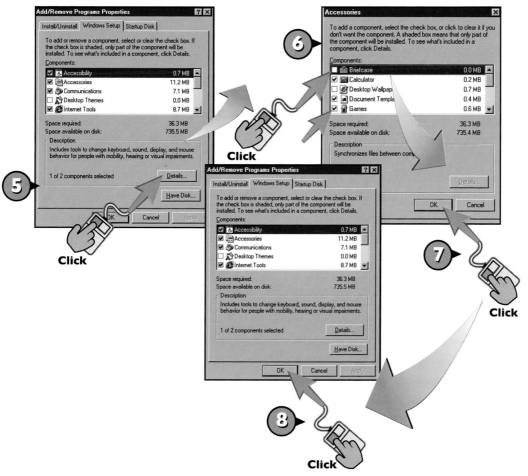

Click

Click

Click

Click

Click

5 ▸ Click the **Details** button.

6 ▸ You see a list of the available programs for this feature. Check the ones that you want to install, and uncheck any you want to uninstall.

7 ▸ Click the **OK** button.

8 ▸ Insert your Windows CD-ROM and click **OK** in the **Windows Setup** tab. Files are copied to your system, and the component is available for use.

Might Want to Install
Some features you might want to install include **Desktop Themes** or **Accessories.**

End Task

Using Windows Accessories

Windows 98 provides several accessories, or applications, that you can use to help you in your work. These accessories are not full-blown programs, but they are useful for specific jobs in the Windows environment. Accessories include a calculator, games, a painting program, a word processor, a text editor, and Internet applications. (The Internet applications are discussed in Part 9, "Connecting to Online Services and the Internet.") Windows 98 also includes some multimedia tools for playing CDs and for recording and playing back sounds. This part covers the basic applications included with Windows 98.

Tasks

Task 1: Playing Games

Windows provides several games that you can play to break up your workday with a little entertainment. Use any of the games to fill a lunch hour or coffee break and to ease the tensions of the day. Playing games is also a good way to help you get the hang of using the mouse. For instance, playing Solitaire can help you practice such mouse skills as clicking, dragging, and so on.

✅ **No Games?**
If you don't see any games listed, they might not have been installed. You can easily add these Windows components to your system (refer to Task 12, "Installing Windows Components," in Part 6, "Setting Up Programs").

✅ **Get Help**
If you aren't sure how to play a game, you can get instructions using the online help. Simply open the **Help** menu and then select **How To Play.**

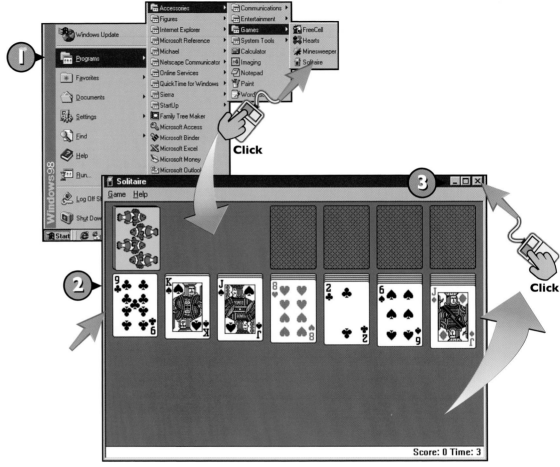

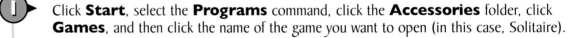

1 ► Click **Start**, select the **Programs** command, click the **Accessories** folder, click **Games**, and then click the name of the game you want to open (in this case, Solitaire).

2 ► Play the game.

3 ► When you are finished, click the **Close** button to exit.

End Task

Task 2: Starting WordPad

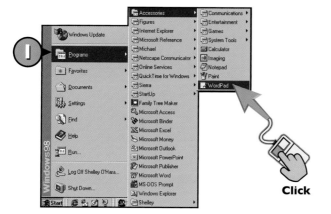

Click

Use WordPad to edit text files, or to create simple documents such as notes, memos, fax sheets, and so on. WordPad saves files in Word 6 for Windows format by default, but you can choose to save in a text-only format.

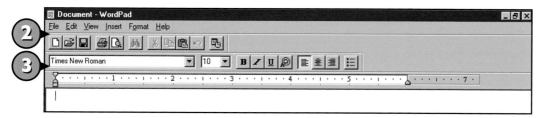

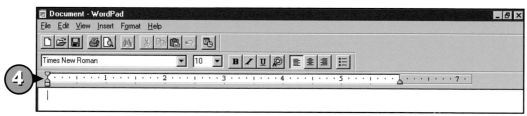

✓ **Maximize the Window**
You can click the **Maximize** button to enlarge the **WordPad** window and make it easier to work in.

✓ **Hide Toolbars**
To hide any of the screen elements in WordPad, open the **View** menu and click the tool you want to hide. A check mark indicates that the tool is showing; no check mark indicates that it is hidden.

① Click **Start**, select the **Programs** command, click the **Accessories** folder, and select **WordPad**.

② Use the menu bar to select commands. Use the toolbar to select buttons for frequently used commands.

③ Use the format bar to make changes to the appearance of the text.

④ Use the ruler for setting tabs and indents.

Task 3: Typing Text

To create a new document, you type the text you want to include. The insertion point indicates where text will be entered as you type.

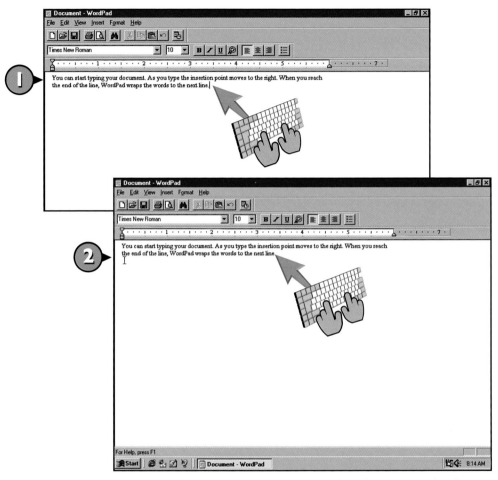

 Type the text. You don't need to press **Enter** at the end of each line; WordPad automatically wraps the lines within a paragraph.

 To end a paragraph and start a new one, press **Enter**. The insertion point moves to the next line.

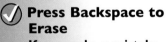 **Press Backspace to Erase**

If you make a mistake while typing, press the **Backspace** key to delete one character at a time. Then retype the text.

Save Your Document

Be sure to periodically save your document. See Task 6, "Saving a Document," in Part 2, "Using Applications in Windows 98."

Task 4: Moving Around in a WordPad Document

Start Here

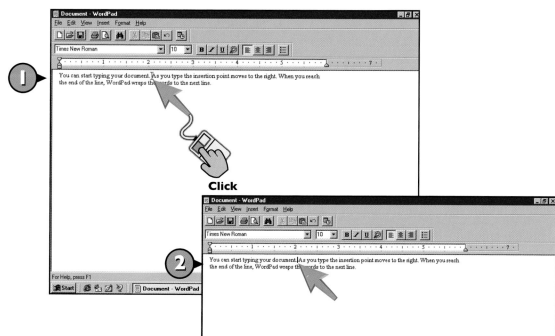

Click

To add new text or to select text for editing or formatting, you need to know how to move the insertion point to the spot where you want to make a change. You can use either the mouse or the keyboard to move the insertion point.

 Point to the spot in the document where you want to place the insertion point, and click the mouse button.

 The insertion point moves to that spot.

✓ Print and Click
Be sure to both point and click. If you simply point, the insertion point is not moved to the new location.

End Task

Task 5: Adding Text

One of the greatest things about using a word-processing program, even a simple program like WordPad, is how easily you can make changes. You can delete text, add text, and more. You can also polish the content of your document, making whatever changes are necessary.

✓ Undo a Change
If you make a mistake, you can undo the last action by clicking the **Edit** menu and choosing **Undo**.

✓ Save Your Work
Be sure to save your document as you continue to work on it. Click **File** and then choose **Save** (or click the **Save** button on the toolbar) to save your work. For more information, refer to Task 6 in Part 2.

✓ Copy or Move Text
For information about copying or moving text, refer to Part 2.

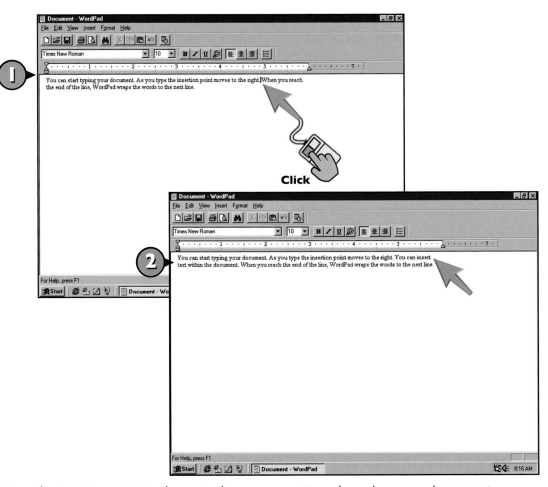

Click

1 Move the insertion point to the spot where you want to make a change, and start typing.

2 The existing text moves over to make room.

End
Task

Task 6: Deleting Text

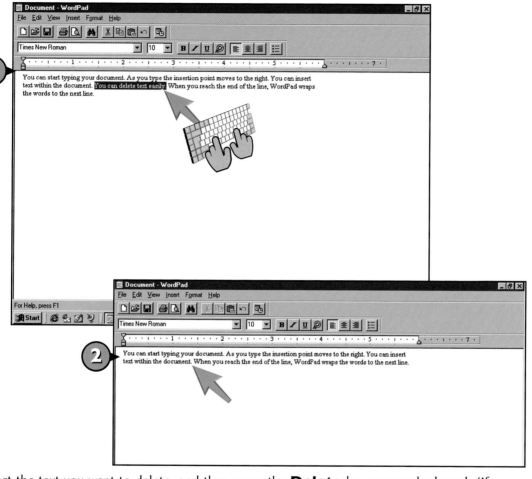

Just as you can add text, you can easily delete it.

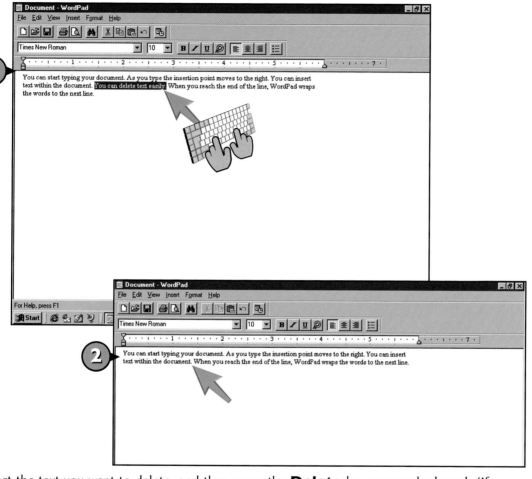 Select the text you want to delete, and then press the **Delete** key on your keyboard. (If you're not sure how to select text, refer to Task II, "Selecting Text," in Part 2.)

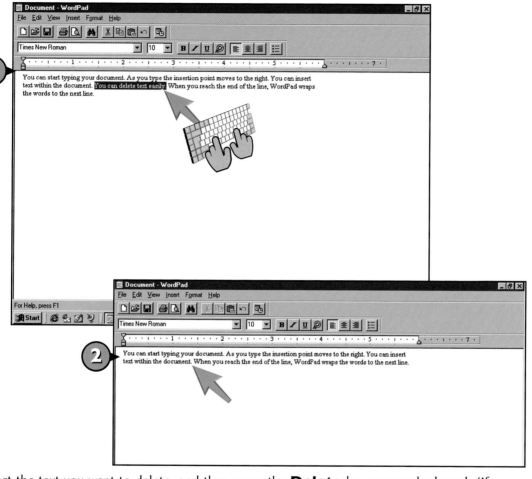 The text is deleted.

✓ Undo Deletion
To undo the deletion, click the Undo button.

Task 7: Formatting Text

You can easily make simple changes to the appearance of the text. For example, you can change the font or font size, and you can make text bold, italic, or underlined. This task touches on just a few of the formatting changes you can make. Experiment to try out some of the other available formatting features.

✓ **Format Paragraphs**
You can use toolbar buttons to change many features of the paragraph. For example, use the **Alignment** buttons to change the alignment of the paragraph. Add bullets by clicking the **Bullets** button. To undo a change, click the **Undo** button. You can also use the commands in the **Format** menu to change the appearance of your document.

Click

Click

 Select the text you want to change. If you need help selecting text, refer to Task 11 in Part 2.

 To use a different font, click the **Font** drop-down arrow and click the font you want.

 To use a different font size, select the text you want to change, click the **Font Size** drop-down arrow, and click the size you want to use.

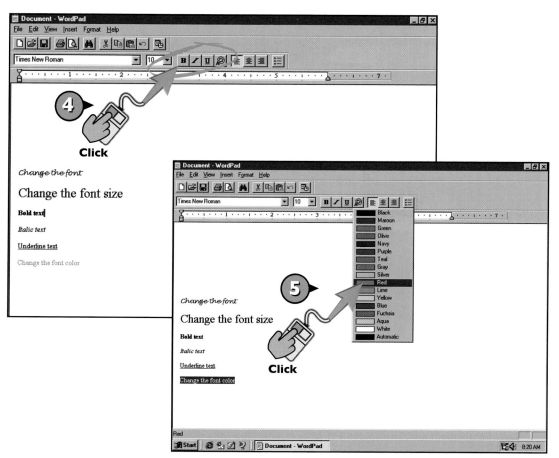

4 To make text bold, italic, or underlined, select the text, and then click the appropriate button in the format bar.

5 To change the font color, select the text you want to change, click the **Font Color** button, and then click the color you want.

 Save Changes
Save your document by clicking the **Save** button or by clicking **File** and then choosing **Save**. For more information on saving a document, refer to Part 2.

End Task

Task 8: Using Notepad

The most common type of simple file is a *text file*. You can find instructions on how to install a program, beta notes, and other information in text files. Some configuration files are also text files. To edit and work with this type of file, you can use Notepad, a simple text editor provided with Windows 98.

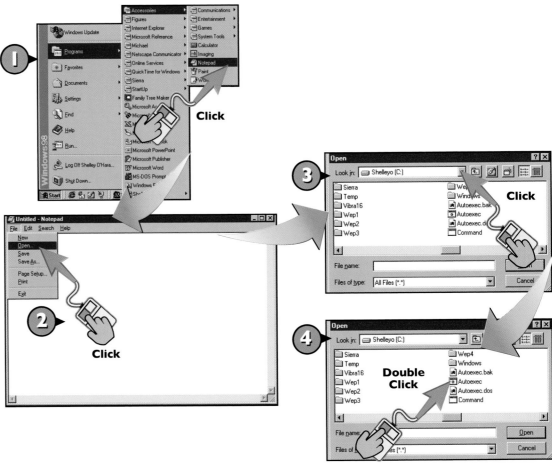

1. Click **Start**, select the **Programs** command, click the **Accessories** folder, and then choose **Notepad**.

2. To open a file in Notepad, click **File** and then choose **Open**.

3. Find the folder that contains your file. You can use the **Look in** drop-down list box to change to a different drive.

4. Double-click the desired folder to open it (in this case, **Autoexec**).

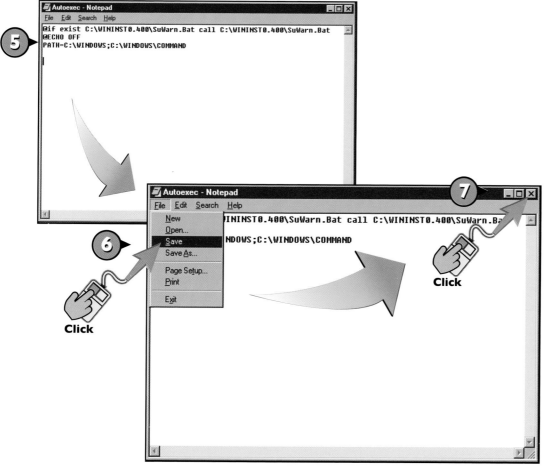

5 ▶ Make any changes to the file.

6 ▶ To save changes to the file, click **File** and then **Save**.

7 ▶ To exit Notepad, click the **Close** button.

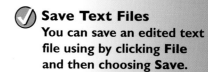

Save Text Files
You can save an edited text file using by clicking **File** and then choosing **Save**.

Task 9: Using Paint

Use Paint to create art and to edit graphics such as clip art, scanned art, and art files from other programs. You can add lines, shapes, and colors, as well as alter the original components.

Click

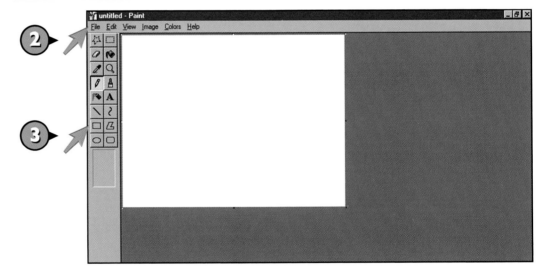

 Experiment!
You can learn more about Paint by experimenting. Also, use the online help system to look up topics.

 Click **Start**, select the **Programs** command, click the **Accessories** folder, and choose **Paint**.

 Use the menu bar to select commands.

3 Use the toolbox to select the drawing tool you want to work with.

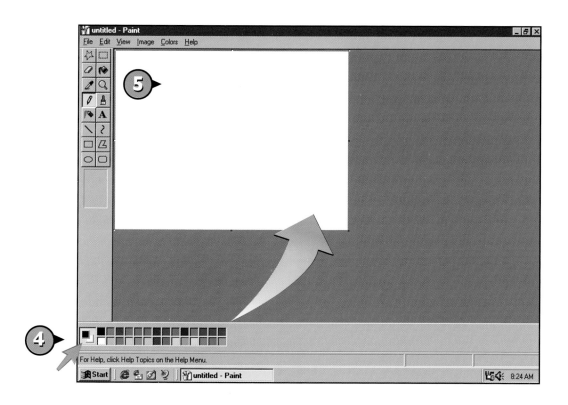

4 ▶ Use the color box to select colors for the lines and fills of the objects you draw.

5 ▶ Draw in the drawing area.

 Draw Shapes
Most drawings consist of shapes. See the next task for help on drawing a shape.

Task 10: Drawing a Shape

You can create many different types of shapes, including lines, curves, rectangles, polygons, ovals, circles, and rounded rectangles.

Start Here

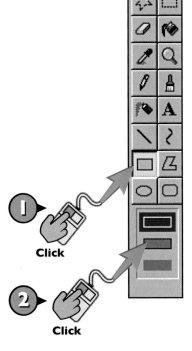

Click

Click

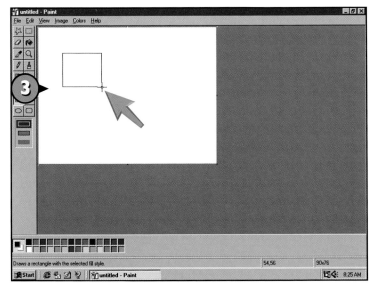

✓ Choose a Color

You can click in the color bar at the bottom of the **Paint** window to choose a color. Click the color you want to use for the lines and borders. To select a fill color, right-click the color you want to use.

✓ Undo

If at any time you do not like what you've drawn, open the **Edit** menu and choose **Undo** to undo the last action.

1 Click the tool you want to draw with (in this case, the **Rectangle** tool).

2 The toolbox displays options for the tool you have selected. In this case, choose whether you want to draw an empty rectangle, a filled rectangle with a border, or a filled rectangle without a border.

3 Move the pointer into the drawing area. Click and drag to draw.

End Task

Task 11: Adding Text to a Drawing

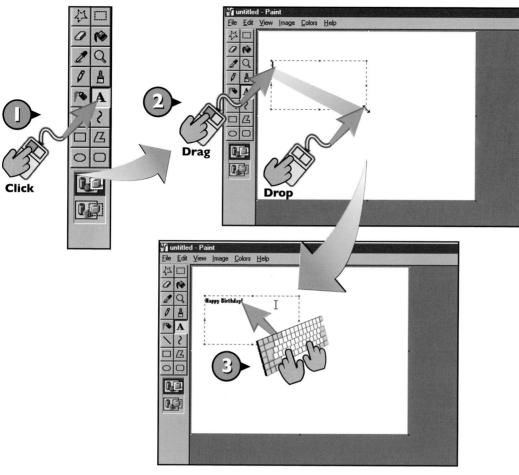

You can include text as part of your drawing. To do so, draw a text box and then type the text you want to include.

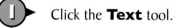 Click the **Text** tool.

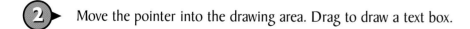 Move the pointer into the drawing area. Drag to draw a text box.

Type the text you want to add. The text is added to the text box.

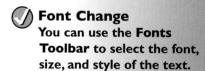 **Font Change**
You can use the **Fonts Toolbar** to select the font, size, and style of the text.

Task 12: Drawing Freehand

In addition to shapes and text, you can also draw freehand on the page. This is similar to drawing with a pencil or pen (only you are drawing in your document!).

Start Here

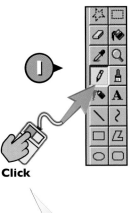

1

Click

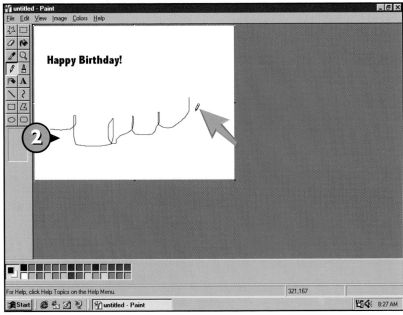

2

1▶ Click the **Pencil** tool.

2▶ Move the pointer into the drawing area. Hold down the mouse button and drag the pencil icon to draw.

End Task

Task 13: Erasing Part of a Drawing

Click

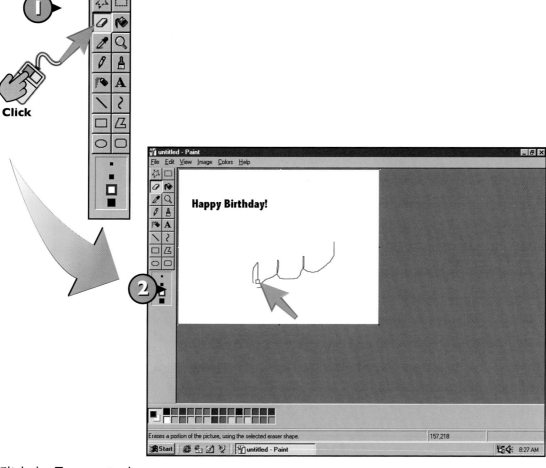

If you make a mistake and want to get rid of something you have added, you can use the **Eraser** tool.

✓ **Erase Selected Area**
To erase a selected part of a drawing, click the **Select** tool and drag the mouse across part of your drawing. Press the **Delete** key to remove the selected part of the drawing.

✓ **Clear Whole Page**
To clear everything on the page, click **Image**, and then choose **Clear Image**.

Click the **Eraser** tool.

Move the pointer to the drawing area. Hold down the mouse button and drag across the part you want to erase.

✓ **Size of the Eraser**
You can select the size of the eraser you want to use. Simply click the **Eraser** tool, and then click the size you want to use in the tool box.

End Task

Task 14: Adding Color to a Drawing Using the Brush Tool

There are many ways to add color to a drawing. One way is to use the **Brush** tool.

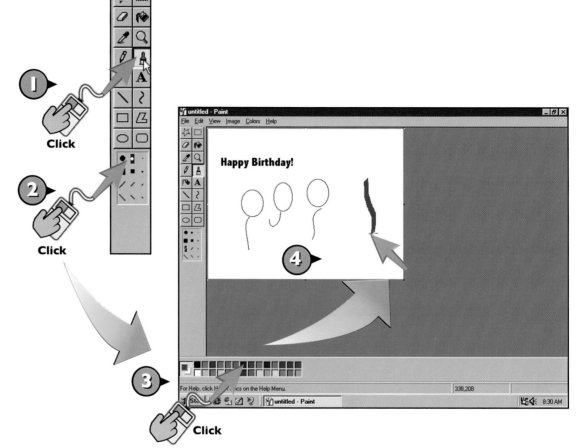

Start Here

Click

Click

Click

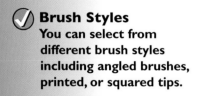

Brush Styles
You can select from different brush styles including angled brushes, printed, or squared tips.

1 ▸ Click the **Brush** tool.

2 ▸ Click the brush size and shape.

3 ▸ Click the color you want to use in the color box.

4 ▸ Hold down the mouse button and drag across the page to "paint" with the brush.

End Task

Task 15: Adding Color to a Drawing Using the Airbrush Tool

You can "spray paint" color onto a page using the **Airbrush** tool. You can select different splatter sizes and also select the color to use.

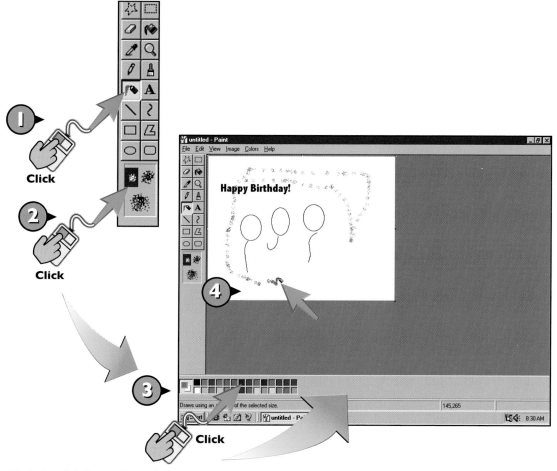

Click

Click

Click

 Click the **Airbrush** tool.

 Click the splatter size you want.

 Click the color you want to use.

 Hold down the mouse button and drag across the page to "spray paint" that color on the page.

You can use the **Fill with Color** tool to fill an object or drawing area with color. For instance, you can fill a rectangle or circle with any of the colors available in the color palette.

Click

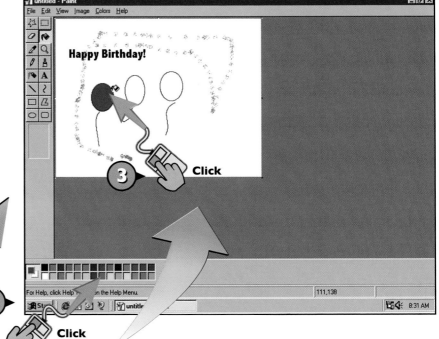

Click

Click

Paint Spills
If color spills outside the area you intended to fill, that probably means you tried to fill an area that was not closed. Be sure that you are filling an area with a border.

Click the **Fill with Color** tool.

Click the color you want to use.

Click inside the area you want to paint. That area is filled with color.

Task 17: Using Calculator

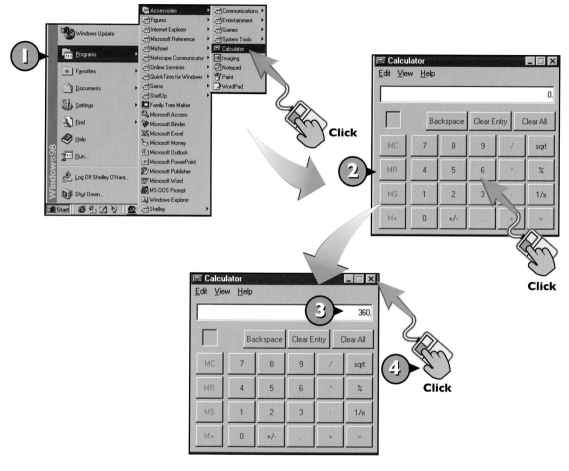

Click

Click

Click

If you need to perform a quick calculation, use the Calculator program included with Windows 98. You can add, subtract, multiply, divide, figure percentages, and more with this handy tool.

✓ **Scientific Calculator**
To use a more complex scientific calculator, click the calculator's **View** menu and then click **Scientific**.

✓ **Copy Results to Document**
You can copy the results of a calculation into a document. To do so, select the results, click **Edit**, and then choose **Copy**. Then move to the document where you want to paste the results, click **Edit**, and then choose **Paste**.

✓ **Use Keypad**
To use the numeric keypad to enter numbers, press the **Num Lock** button. Then type the equation using these keys.

1 ▶ Click **Start**, select the **Programs** command, choose the **Accessories** folder, and then click **Calculator**.

2 ▶ Click the buttons on the calculator to enter an equation.

3 ▶ You see the results of the calculation.

4 ▶ When you are finished, click the **Close** button.

Task 18: Playing a Sound with Sound Recorder

You can use various Windows multimedia devices, such as the Sound Recorder, to add to the presentations or documents you create in Windows. Use Sound Recorder to record your own sounds and insert the sound files into your documents for clarification or interest. To use the multimedia features of Windows 98, you need a sound card and speakers.

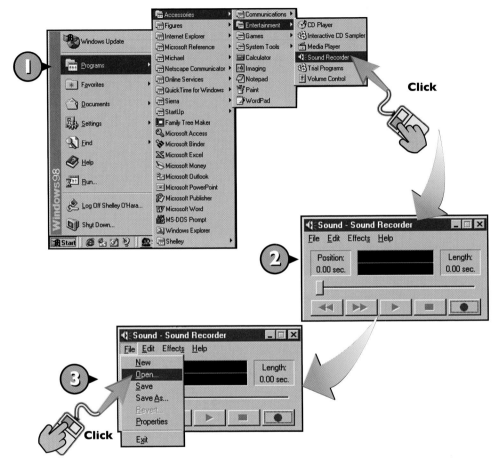

✓ Record a Sound

You can record sounds using Sound Recorder. To do so, you must have an audio input device (microphone) attached to your PC. Click **File**, choose **New**, and then click the **Record** button and record your sound. To stop recording, click the **Stop** button. To save your sound, click **File** and then choose **Save As**.

✓ Can't Hear?

If you cannot hear the sound, adjust the volume on your speakers.

1 ▶ Click **Start**, select the **Programs** command, choose the **Accessories** folder, click the **Entertainment** folder, and select **Sound Recorder**.

2 ▶ The **Sound Recorder** window appears. Its buttons resemble the buttons on a tape recorder. Use these buttons to play back a sound.

3 ▶ Click the **File** menu, and then choose **Open**.

Next Step

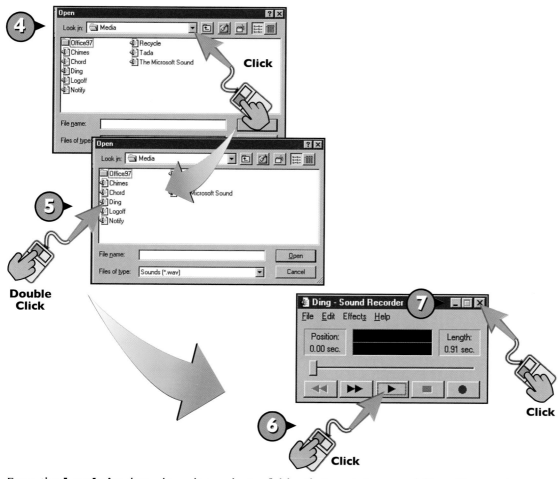

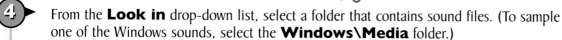

4 ▶ From the **Look in** drop-down list, select a folder that contains sound files. (To sample one of the Windows sounds, select the **Windows\Media** folder.)

5 ▶ Double-click the sound file you want to play.

6 ▶ Click the **Play** button.

7 ▶ Click the **Close** button to close the **Sound Recorder** window.

Task 19: Playing an Audio CD

In addition to being able to play back sound files, you can play audio CDs using **CD Player**, enabling you to listen to the background music of your choice as you work. Note that in order to use the multimedia features of Windows 98, you need a sound card and speakers.

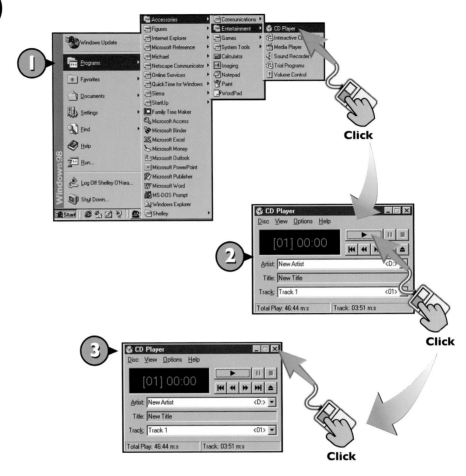

Click

Click

Click

✓ **Auto Play**
If you insert a CD, CD Player will start automatically.

✓ **Stop Play**
To stop playing, click the **Stop** button. To close the **CD Player** window and exit CD Player, click the **Close** button.

✓ **Play Different Track**
To play a different track, display the **Track** drop-down list and select the track you want to play.

1 ▶ Click **Start**, select the **Programs** command, choose the **Accessories** folder, click the **Entertainment** folder, and choose **CD Player**.

2 ▶ After you insert your CD into your CD drive, click the **Play** button in the **CD Player** window.

3 ▶ When you're finished, click the **Close** button to close the **CD Player** window.

Task 20: Changing the Volume

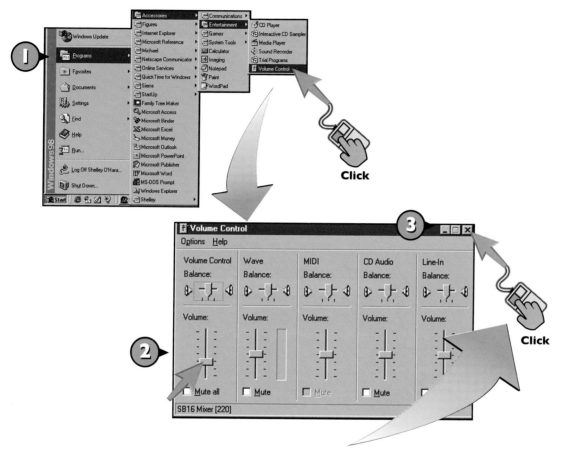

Click

Click

To adjust the volume of
your multimedia programs,
use **Volume Control**.

---

①▶ Click **Start**, select the **Programs** command, choose the **Accessories** folder, click
the **Entertainment** folder, and select **Volume Control**.

②▶ Drag any of the volume control bars in the **Volume Control** window to adjust the
volume.

③▶ Click the **Close** button to close Volume Control.

✔ **Speaker Volume**
You might also have a
volume control on your
speakers. You can also use
these to adjust the sound.

✔ **Double-Click Icon**
To display the **Volume
Control** panel, you can
also double-click the
Speaker icon in the
taskbar.

Task 21: Playing a Media File

Media files are a combination of text, graphics, sounds, video, and animations. Windows 98 comes with some sample media files. To play these presentations, you can use Media Player.

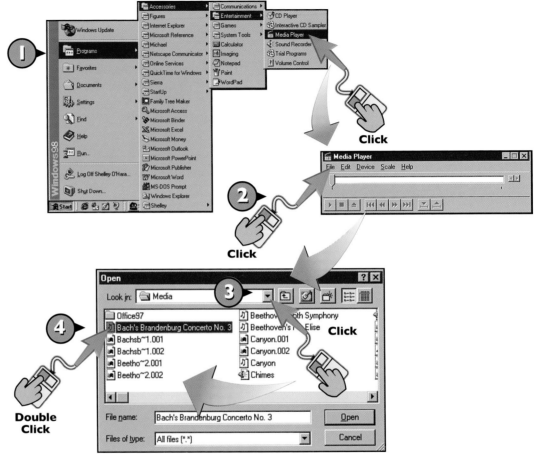

✅ No Sample Media Files?

If you have no media files available, it might be because these files were not installed when Windows was set up. You can add other components, including sample media files. See Task 12, "Installing Windows Components," in Part 6 of this book.

✅ Internet Media

The Internet includes many types of media files. For information on browsing the Internet, see Part 9, "Connecting to Online Services and the Internet."

1 ▶ Click **Start**, select the **Programs** command, choose the **Accessories** folder, click the **Entertainment** folder, and select **Media Player**.

2 ▶ In the **Media Player** window, click **File** and then choose **Open**.

3 ▶ In the **Look in** drop-down list box, search for a folder that contains media files. (To sample one of the Windows media files, open the **Windows\Media** folder.)

4 ▶ Double-click the file you want to play.

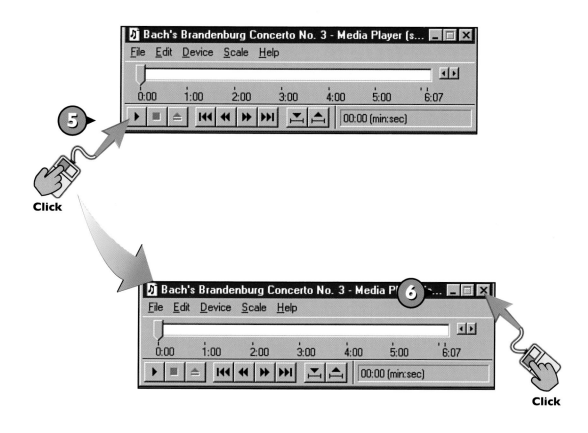

Click

Click

5 ▸ Click the **Play** button.

6 ▸ To close Media Player, click the **Close** button

End Task

Maintaining Your System

This part of the book introduces some techniques that are useful for maintaining your system: defragmenting a disk, backing up data files, scanning a disk for damage, and others.

To safeguard your data files, you should periodically make an extra copy, called a *backup*. You can use the backup program included with Windows 98 to make backup easy.

Tasks

Task 1: Displaying Disk Information

You can display information about your disks, such as the size, the amount of space taken, and the amount of free space. You can also enter a label for a disk; this label is used in file windows to identify the disk.

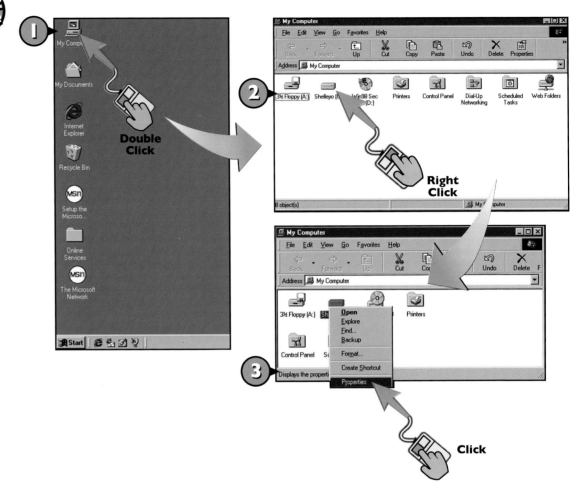

✓ **System Tools**
Use the **Tools** tab to select different programs for maintaining your system. This part covers most of the tools found under this tab.

✓ **Single-Click in Web View**
If you are working in Web view, you can single-click **My Computer** to display its contents.

1 ▸ Double-click the **My Computer** icon.

2 ▸ In the **My Computer** window, right-click the disk for which you want information.

3 ▸ Click **Properties**.

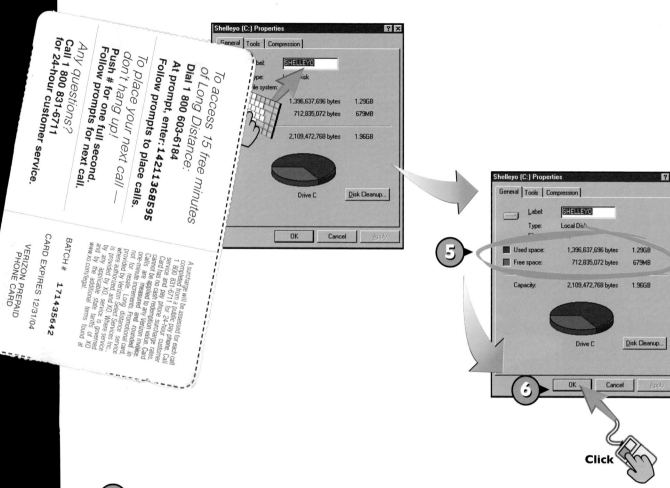

Click

4 If you want, enter a disk label in the **Label** field.

5 View information about used and free space.

6 Click the **OK** button to close the dialog box.

Clean Up Files
For information on getting rid of files with Disk Cleanup, see Task 4.

Task 2: Scanning Your Disk for Errors

Sometimes parts of your hard disk get damaged, and you might see an error message when you try to open or save a file or you might notice lost or disarrayed data in some of your files. You can scan the disk for damage using the ScanDisk program and fix any problems. You must also run ScanDisk before you can defragment a hard disk (covered next).

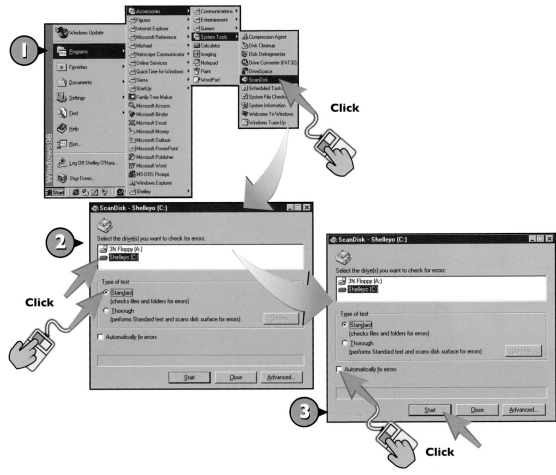

Click

Click

Click

Start Here

✓ Difference Between Tests

The main difference between the two tests is that the Thorough ScanDisk test methodically checks each sector of the disk in detail, and takes up to four times as long to complete as the Standard. Try the Standard first; if it finds problems it cannot fix, then perform the Thorough test.

1 Click **Start**, choose the **Programs** command, select the **Accessories** folder, click the **System Tools** folder, and choose **ScanDisk**.

2 In the **ScanDisk** dialog box, select the drive you want to scan. In the **Type of test** section, click the radio button next to the type of test you want (**Standard** or **Thorough**).

3 Specify whether you want ScanDisk to automatically fix errors by checking or unchecking the **Automatically fix errors** check box, then click **Start**.

Next Step

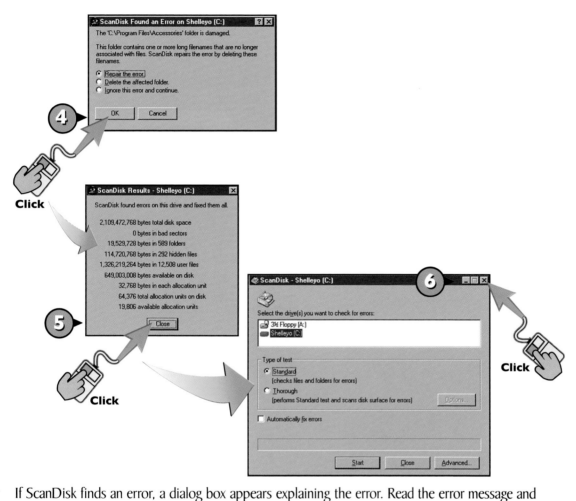

Click

Click

Click

Click

(4) If ScanDisk finds an error, a dialog box appears explaining the error. Read the error message and choose the option that best suits your needs. Click **OK** to continue. Do this for each message.

(5) When ScanDisk finishes, it displays a report of the scan. Click **Close** to return to the **ScanDisk** dialog box.

(6) Click the **Close** button to exit ScanDisk.

✔ **ScanDisk Runs Automatically**
If you don't properly shut down Windows, you are prompted to run ScanDisk when you reboot. You can then check for errors before your system is restarted.

✔ **No ScanDisk?**
If ScanDisk is not listed on the **System Tools** menu, this program may not have been installed when you installed Windows. See Task 12, "Installing Windows Components" in Part 6, "Setting Up Programs."

End Task

Task 3: Defragmenting a Disk

When a file is stored on your hard drive, Windows places as much of the file as possible in the first available section (called a *cluster*) and then goes to the next cluster to put the next part of the file. Initially, this storage does not cause performance problems, but over time, your disk files become *fragmented*; you might find that it takes a long time to open a file or start a program. To speed access to files and to help prevent potential problems with fragmented files, you can defragment your disk, putting files in clusters as close to each other as possible. Defragmenting your disk is a general-maintenance job that you should perform every few months for best results.

✓ **Defrag Not Needed?**
If the disk does not need to be defragmented, Windows displays a message stating that. You can exit or you can defragment anyway.

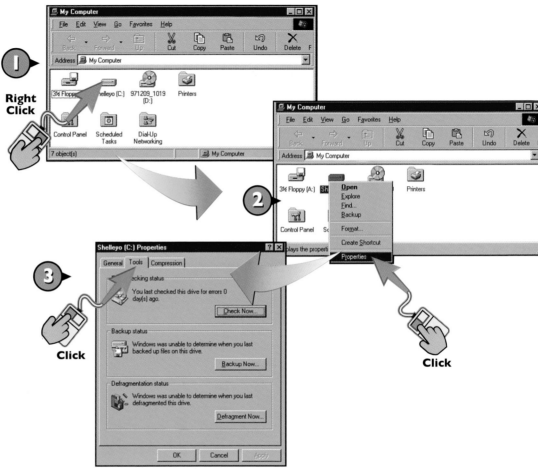

In the **My Computer** window, right-click the disk you want to defragment.

Click **Properties**.

Click the **Tools** tab.

Next Step

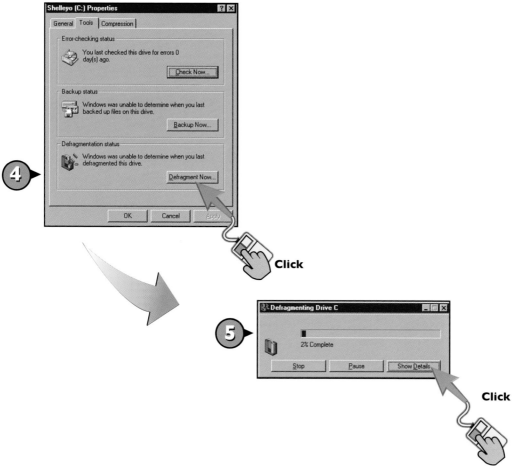

Click

Click

Back Up Files
Be careful when defragmenting. You might want to back up first. See Task 5 for information about backing up.

When Defrag Is Done
When the Defragmenter finishes, a dialog box notifies you that it is done and asks if you want to quit Disk Defragmenter. Click **Yes** to quit or choose **No** to return to the **Select Drive** dialog box and defragment another disk.

4 ▶ Click the **Defragment Now** button.

5 ▶ The Defragmenter's progress is indicated by the progress bar in the **Defragmenting** dialog box. You can stop or pause the defragmenting at any time by clicking the appropriate button. To display details of the progress, click the **Show Details** button.

Task 4: Cleaning Up Unnecessary Files

On your system, unnecessary files may be hogging your disk space. Programs such as Internet Explorer store temporary files on your system that you can delete. The **Recycle Bin** also houses files that you have deleted, but are still kept in case you need them. You can easily get rid of these files and gain some disk space.

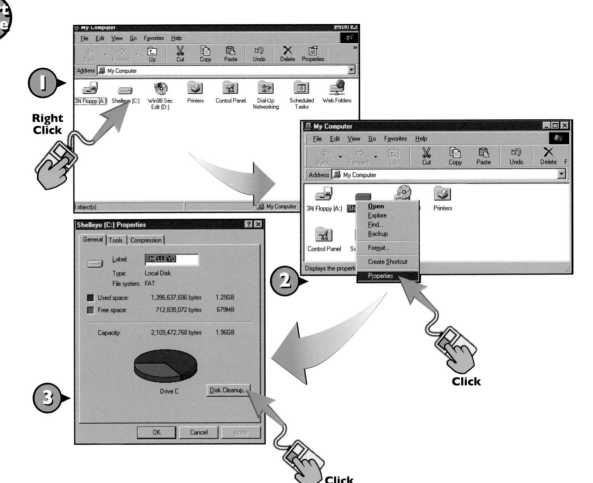

Right Click

Click

Click

✓ View Files

You can view the files that are recommended for removal. Select the files you want to view and then click the **View Files** button.

✓ Be Careful

Be sure you don't need any of these files. Once they are removed, you cannot get them back.

1. In the **My Computer** window, right-click the disk you want to work with.

2. Click **Properties**.

3. Click the **Disk Cleanup** button. Windows calculates the space you can save and displays a list of files recommended for removal.

Next Step

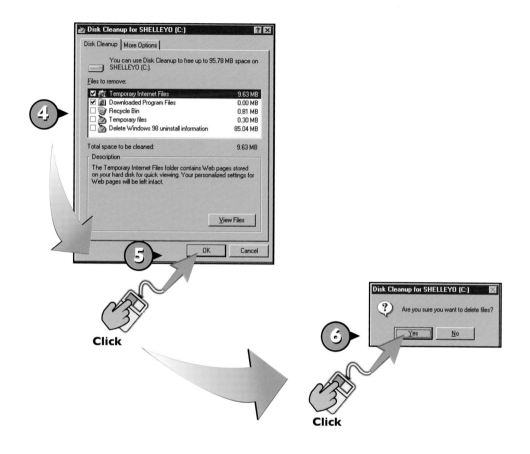

4 ▶ Review the list and check any files you want removed. Uncheck any files you don't want removed.

5 ▶ Click the **OK** button.

6 ▶ When prompted to confirm the removal, click the **Yes** button.

✅ **Close Dialog Box**
After cleaning up the files, click the **Close (x)** button to close the dialog box.

❗ **Check Files**
Be sure to check the files carefully. Once they are removed, you cannot undelete them.

Task 5: Backing Up All Files on Your Computer

Start Here

To safeguard your data, back up the files on your system. That way, if something happens to the original, you can restore with this backup or an extra copy. The first time you do a backup, you might want to back up all the files on your system. After you have a complete backup, you can then back up only selected files. Windows includes a backup program you can use. This task covers how to back up all files. The next one covers how to back up selected files.

✓ **Start from Tools Tab**
You can start the backup program from the **Tools** tab in the **Disk Properties** dialog box.

✓ **Tape Backups**
If backup is critical to your system, you might want to purchase a tape backup system. This method is faster and more convenient than backing up to floppy disks or to a disk file.

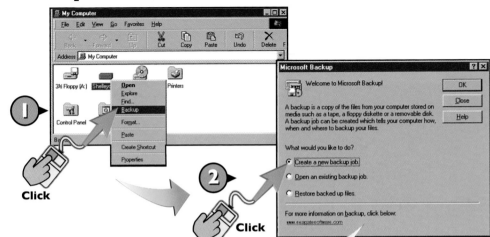

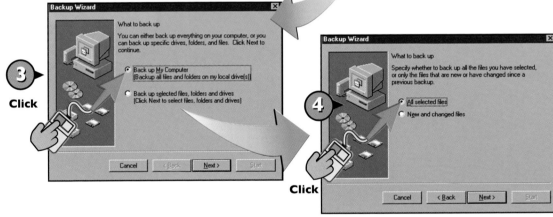

Click

Click

Click

Click

 In the **My Computer** window, right-click the disk you want to back up, and then click **Backup**.

 Select the **Create a new backup job** radio button, and then click **OK**.

Select the **Back up My Computer** radio button, and then click the **Next** button.

 Specify whether you want to back up all files or only new and changed files, and then click the **Next** button.

Next Step

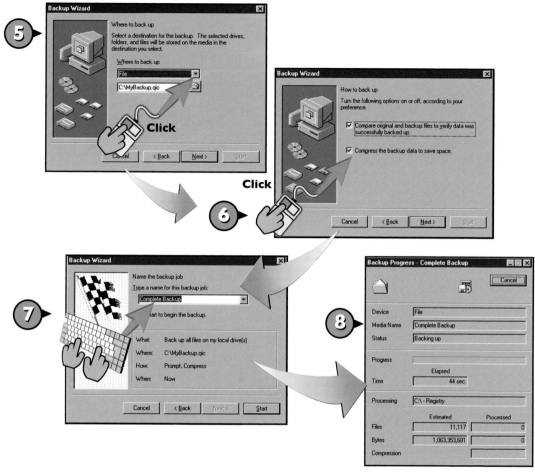

Set Up Backup Devices
The first time you run backup, you are prompted to set up any backup devices you have. Follow the onscreen instructions.

Go Back a Step
You can click the **Back** button to go back and make a change to your selections. Click the **Cancel** button to stop the backup.

Progress of Backup
The **Backup Progress** dialog box displays the time elapsed, the files processed, the compression statistics, and other information.

5 ▶ Select a destination for the backup—the default is **File**—and then click the **Next** button.

6 ▶ Specify whether backup files are compared and verified and whether the backup data is compressed, and then click **Next**.

7 ▶ Type a name for the backup set (to help you keep track of different backups you make of your system) and then click **Start**.

8 ▶ Watch the backup's progress in the **Backup Progress** dialog box. After you get a message indicating that the backup is complete, click **OK**.

Task 6: Backing Up Selected Files

You should set up a backup routine that suits you. You might want to back up daily, weekly, or monthly, depending on how often your data is changed and how difficult it would be to recover that data if it was lost. Once you've done a complete backup, you can then back up selected files (all files that have changed, all files in a particular folder, all files of a certain type, and so on). This task explains how to select which files are backed up.

✓ **Start Backup**
Refer to Task 5 if you need help opening the **Microsoft Backup** dialog box.

✓ **Schedule Backup**
You can schedule tasks such as Backup as a reminder to perform them on a regular basis. For information on scheduling tasks, see Task 10, "Scheduling Tasks," later in this part.

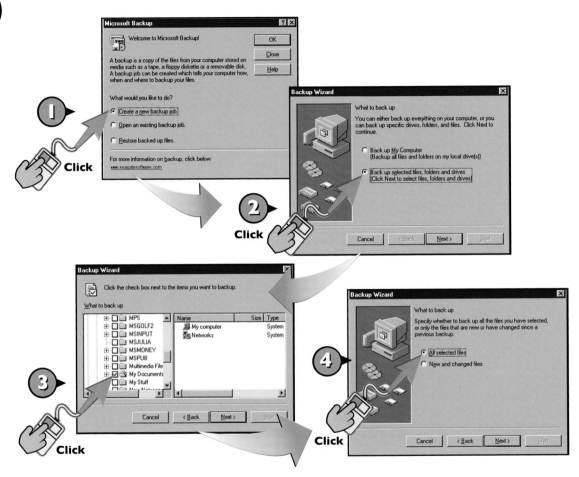

After you open the **Microsoft Backup** dialog, select the **Create a new backup job** radio button and then click **OK**.

Select the **Back up selected files, folders and drives** option, and then click the **Next** button.

Check the items you want to back up, and then click the **Next** button.

Specify whether to back up all files or only new and changed files, and then click the **Next** button.

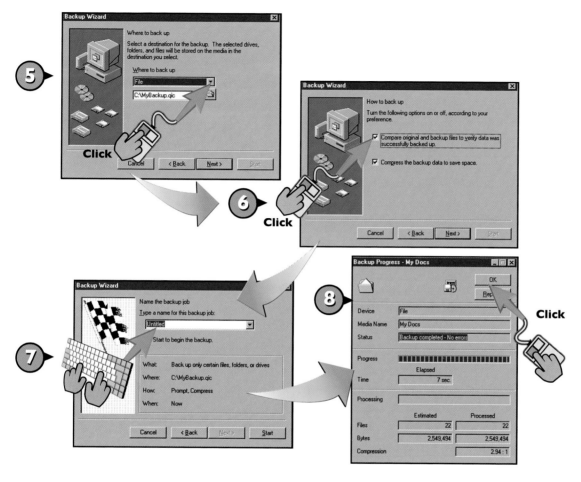

 Select a destination for the backup, and then click the **Next** button.

 Select backup options—whether the backup files are compared and verified and whether the backup data is compressed—and then click **Next**.

 Type a name for the backup set, and then click the **Start** button.

 Click the **OK** button in the **Backup Progress** dialog when you see the message indicating that the operation is complete.

✅ **Expand List**
If necessary, click the plus signs next to the drive and folders to display the folder(s) you want to back up.

✅ **Backup Progress**
The **Backup Progress** dialog box displays the time elapsed, the files processed, the compression statistics, and other information.

Task 7: Restoring a Backup

Backup files are stored in a special format. You can't simply copy these files from the backup disks to your hard disk; you must use a special restore procedure. You can restore any files from any of your backup sets.

✓ **Get Backup Set**
Before you start a restore, make sure you have the disks or tapes with the backup set.

✓ **Placing Files**
When you restore, you can elect to place the files in the same location or in a different location. You can also select how to handle files that are the same. Keep in mind that the restored files will overwrite the original files.

✓ **Start Backup**
Refer to Task 5 if you need help opening the **Microsoft Backup** dialog box.

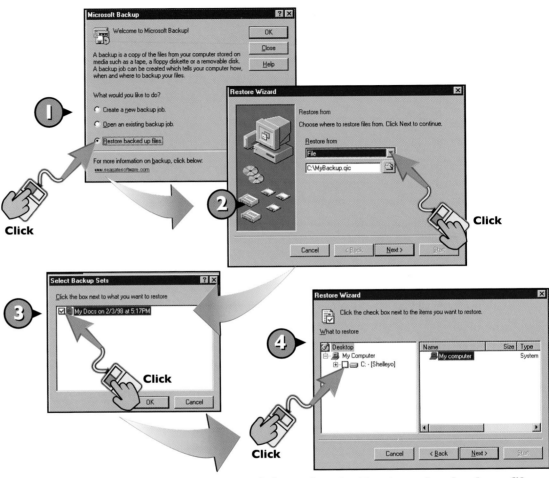

Click

Click

Click

Click

1 ▶ After you open the **Microsoft Backup** dialog, select the **Restore backed up files** radio button and then click **OK**.

2 ▶ Select where to restore from—that is, where you stored the drive or folder that contains the backup files—and then click **Next**.

3 ▶ Select the backup set, and then click the **OK** button.

4 ▶ Check the items you want to restore, and then click the **Next** button.

Next Step

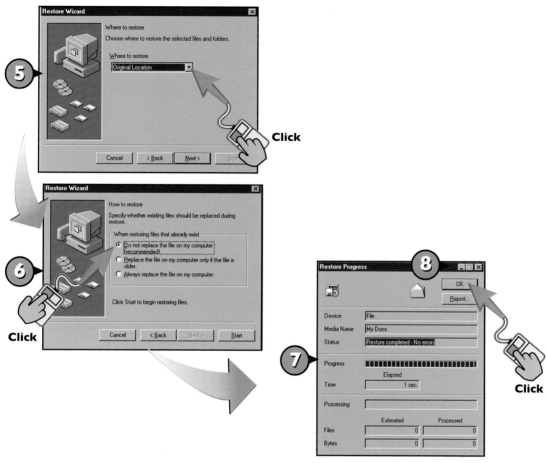

5 Specify where to place the restored files, and then click the **Next** button.

6 Select how restored files should be handled, and then click the **Start** button.

7 The files are restored; the progress of the restore operation is visible in the **Restore Progress** dialog.

8 When the restore is complete, you see a message. Click the **OK** button.

✅ **Restore Progress**
The Restore Progress dialog displays the time elapsed, the files processed, compression statistics, and other information.

Task 8: Formatting a Disk

To be able to use a floppy disk, the disk must be formatted. Many disks sold are already formatted, but if they are not or if you want to reformat a disk, you can do so. Keep in mind that formatting a disk erases all the information on that disk.

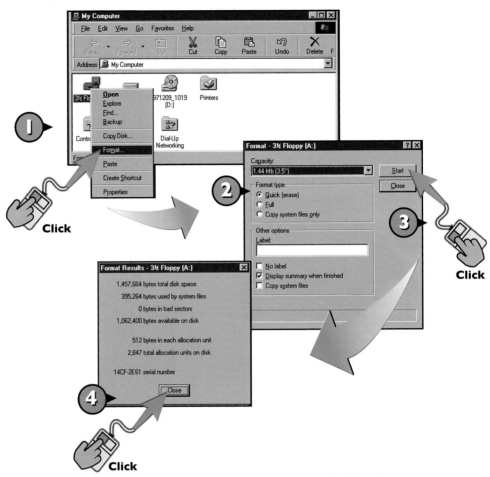

✓ **Don't Format Your Hard Disk**
You want to format a hard disk only in the most extreme circumstances. Remember that formatting a disk erases all information on that disk. If you format your hard disk, everything on it will be wiped out.

✓ **Startup Disk**
For information on creating a startup disk to use to start your system, see the next task.

1 After you've inserted a floppy disk into the drive, open the **My Computer** window. Right-click the floppy disk drive, and choose **Format**.

2 Make any changes in the **Capacity** and **Format type** sections (and type a label for the disk if you want).

3 Click **Start**.

4 Windows formats the disk and displays a message with details about the disk. To exit, click the **Close** button twice.

Task 9: Creating a Startup Disk

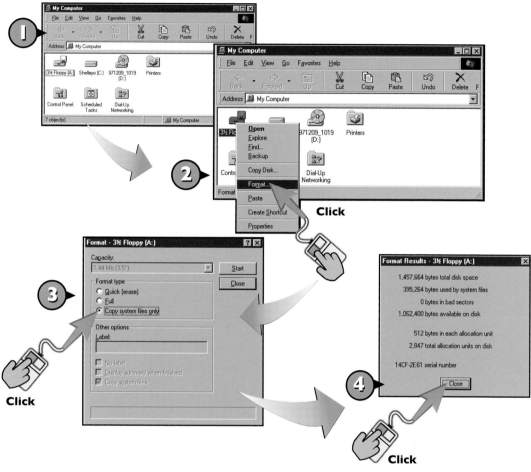

Click

Click

Click

When you start up your system, it looks for the appropriate startup files on the floppy drive and then goes to the hard drive. This startup method ensures that if something is wrong with the hard drive, you can always start from a floppy disk. You can make a startup disk with the necessary files to keep for emergencies.

1 After inserting a floppy disk into the drive, open the **My Computer** window.

2 Right-click the floppy disk drive, and choose **Format**.

3 Check the **Copy system files only** check box, and then click the **Start** button.

4 Windows formats the disk and displays a message with details about the disk. Click the **Close** button twice.

✓ **Use a Blank Disk**
Be sure to use a blank floppy disk or a floppy disk that doesn't contain anything you need. When you create the startup disk, all other information on the disk you use will be erased.

End Task

Task 10: Scheduling Tasks

If you perform the same tasks repeatedly, or if you often forget to perform routine maintenance tasks, you can set up a schedule that instructs Windows to perform these tasks automatically.

✓ **Double-Click Icon**
You can also double-click the **Scheduled Tasks** icon in the taskbar to display the **Scheduled Tasks** list.

✓ **Remove a Task**
To remove a task from the list, display the list. Right-click the item and then choose **Delete**. Confirm the deletion by clicking the **Yes** button.

✓ **Change Tasks**
To change the settings for the task (the time, interval, name, and so on), display the **Scheduled Task** list. Right-click the item you want to modify and then choose **Properties**. Make any changes to the tabs in the **Properties** dialog box and then click **OK**.

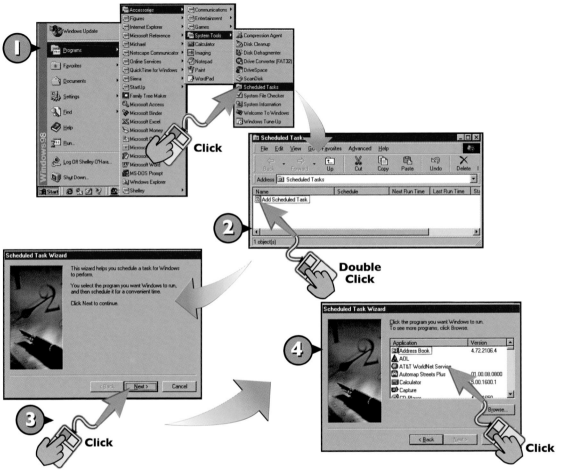

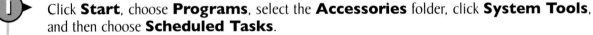

1. ► Click **Start**, choose **Programs**, select the **Accessories** folder, click **System Tools**, and then choose **Scheduled Tasks**.

2. ► Double-click the **Add Scheduled Task** list item.

3. ► Click the **Next** button.

4. ► Select the name of the program that you want Windows to run, and then click the **Next** button.

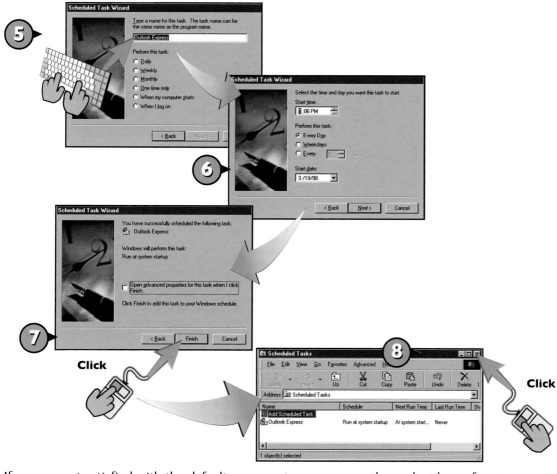

Click

Click

5 If you are not satisfied with the default name, enter a new one; then select how often to perform this task. Click **Next**.

6 If prompted, enter the time and date to start. (Depending on how often you select to perform this task, you might not have to enter the start time and date.)

7 Click the **Finish** button.

8 The task is added. Click the **Close** button to close the **Scheduled Tasks** window.

 Tasks Listed
If you have already set up tasks, they are listed in the **Scheduled Tasks** window. If you have not, you can add one.

 End Task

Task 11: Installing New Hardware

You can install a new printer, modem, or other hardware quickly and easily by using Windows' wizard feature. Windows guides you through questions about the hardware, and if you do not know the answers, Windows can detect the type of hardware and install it with little input from you. Windows calls this handy feature *Plug-and-Play*. This task shows you how to install hardware.

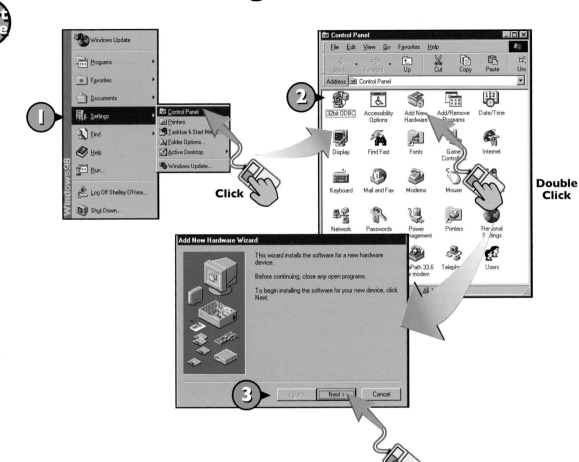

Not Detected?

If the hardware is not automatically detected, you can select to install it manually. Select **No, the device isn't in the list.** Click **Next** and follow the onscreen instructions.

Cancel Setup

You can choose **Cancel** at any time to stop the process. Click **Back** to go back and change a selection you made.

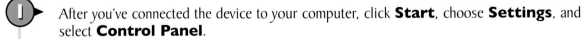

1. After you've connected the device to your computer, click **Start**, choose **Settings**, and select **Control Panel**.

2. Double-click the **Add New Hardware** icon.

3. Click the **Next** button.

Next Step

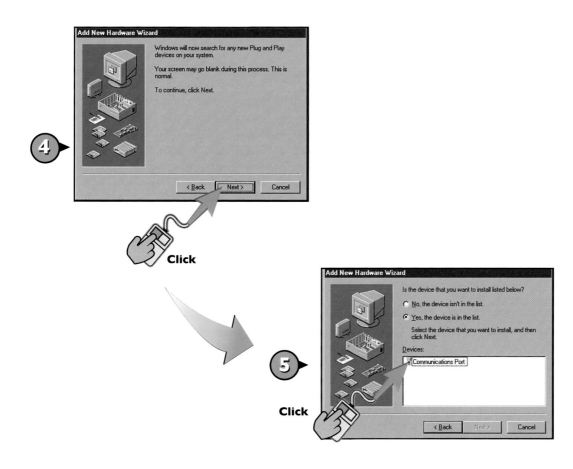

Click

Click

4 Click the **Next** button.

5 Windows searches your system and displays newly installed hardware. Select the device to install from the **Devices** list, and then click **Next**.

✓ **Connect Hardware**
Connect the new hardware device to your computer by following the instructions that came with the hardware device.

✓ **Detected Automatically**
If Windows detected your hardware, it is set up automatically. You may be prompted to insert the appropriate software disks to set up the hardware. Follow the onscreen directions.

Task 12: Displaying System Properties

When you are troubleshooting, you sometimes need to display information about your system. You can find this information in the **Properties** dialog box for **My Computer**.

Start Here

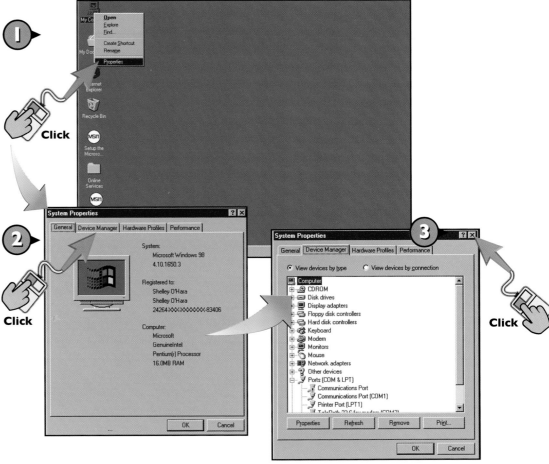

Click

Click

Click

Right-click the **My Computer** icon and choose **Properties**.

You see the **General** tab. Click any of the other tabs to display specific system information.

When you are finished, click the **Close** button.

End Task

Task 13: Viewing System Information

Start Here

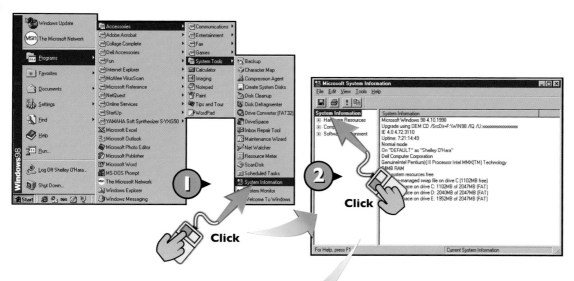

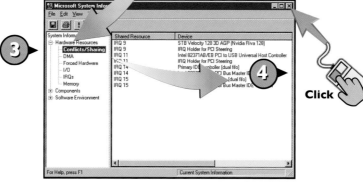

You can use the **System Information** window to view system information as well as check system files.

End Task

① ► Click **Start**, choose **Programs**, select the **Accessories** folder, click **System Tools**, and then choose **System Information**.

② ► You see the **System Information** window. To display information about another listed item (in this case, **Hardware Resources**), click it.

③ ► Information about the entry that you clicked in step 2 appears.

④ ► When you are finished, click the **Close (x)** button for the System Information window.

✓ **Check System Files**
See the next task for help on checking system files.

Task 14: Checking System Files

Windows runs certain system files during startup. If these files get damaged, you can check and repair them using the System Information tools.

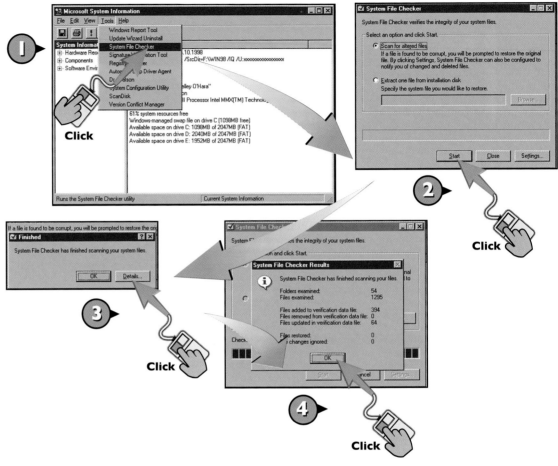

 Click

 Click

 Click

 Click

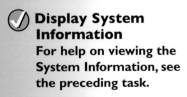

✓ **Display System Information**
For help on viewing the System Information, see the preceding task.

1 From the **System Information** window, click the **Tools** menu and select **System File Checker**.

2 Select **Scan for altered files** and click the **Start** button.

3 When the check is completed, you see a message box. To see a list of files and folders checked and restored, click **Details**.

4 Review this information and then click **OK** or **Close (x)** to close all open windows.

Task 15: Running the Maintenance Wizard

Start
Here

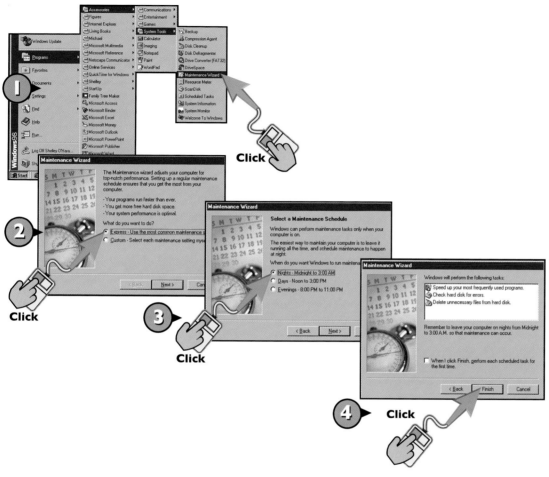

Click

Click

Click

Click

Included new with Windows 98 is the **Maintenance wizard.** You can use this program to handle maintenance tasks such as deleting unnecessary files, checking your hard disk, and speeding up frequently used programs.

 1 Click **Start**, choose **Programs**, select the **Accessories** folder, click **System Tools**, and then choose **Maintenance Wizard**.

 2 Select the **Express** radio button and click **Next**.

 3 Select a time to run the maintenance tasks and click **Next**.

 4 Click the **Finish** button.

 Custom Maintenance
For more control over what tasks are performed, select the **Custom** method and follow the onscreen instructions for making your selections.

Connecting to Online Services and the Internet

If you have a modem and an Internet connection, you can venture beyond your PC to resources available from online services, such as America Online and MSN, or from the Internet. Windows 98 comes with an **Online Services** folder; you can use the icons in this program to try out any of these services. Windows 98 also includes Internet Explorer 4, a Web browser that offers you complete and convenient browsing of the Internet. As with any browser software, you can use Internet Explorer to view World Wide Web pages, to search for specific topics, and to download and upload files. In addition to browsing the Web, you can use Internet Explorer 4's mail program, Outlook Express, to exchange email messages with others who are connected to the Internet. You can also use Outlook Express to participate in newsgroups.

Tasks

America Online (AOL) is the most popular online service company. AOL provides content, bulletin boards, email, and other services for subscribers. You can also access the Internet through AOL. Windows 98 conveniently enables you to try out America Online; you can find the **AOL** icon in the **Online Services** folder on your desktop.

✅ **Cancel Setup**
You can cancel the setup at any time by clicking the **Cancel** button.

✅ **Trial Subscription**
Most online providers offer a trial subscription. After that subscription expires, you must pay for the service. Be sure you understand all the fees involved before you sign up.

✅ **Get More Info**
To review information about the online services, double-click the **About the Online Services** icon. Close the informational window by clicking its **Close** button.

Task 1: Connecting to America Online

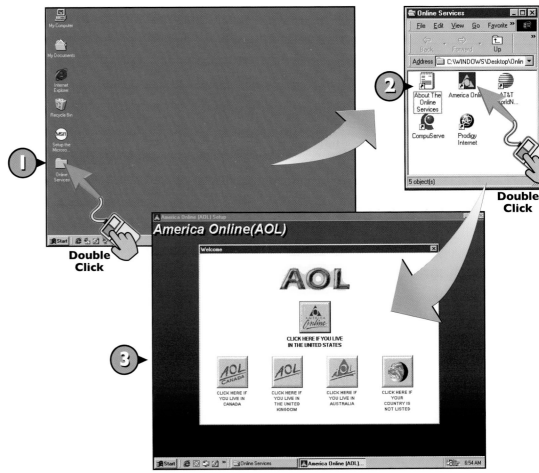

1 Double-click the **Online Services** folder.

2 To set up America Online, double-click the **America Online** icon.

3 Follow the onscreen instructions for getting set up.

Task 2: Connecting to MSN

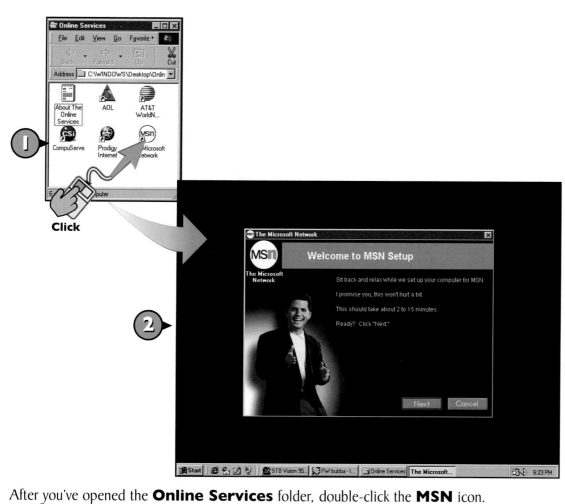

Click

Another popular online service provider is **Microsoft Network (MSN)**, which is managed by Microsoft. Like America Online, **MSN** enables you to view content, participate in forums and other types of discussions (such as live chats), send email, and access the Internet. You can find information about this online service provider in the **Online Services** folder.

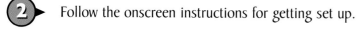

After you've opened the **Online Services** folder, double-click the **MSN** icon.

Follow the onscreen instructions for getting set up.

✓ **Have Your Windows Disc**
If you did not install MSN when you set up Windows, you will be prompted to insert your Windows 98 disc. Be sure you have it handy.

✓ **Opening Folder**
Refer to the previous task if you need help opening the **Online Services** folder.

Task 3: Setting Up for the Internet

Start Here

To explore the Internet, you must have a modem and an Internet connection. You can get this connection through online providers such as America Online or MSN, or you can get an account from an independent Internet service provider (ISP). Before you can take advantage of all the benefits of the Internet, you have to get your Internet connection set up. Windows makes it easy to set up by providing a wizard that guides you through the steps.

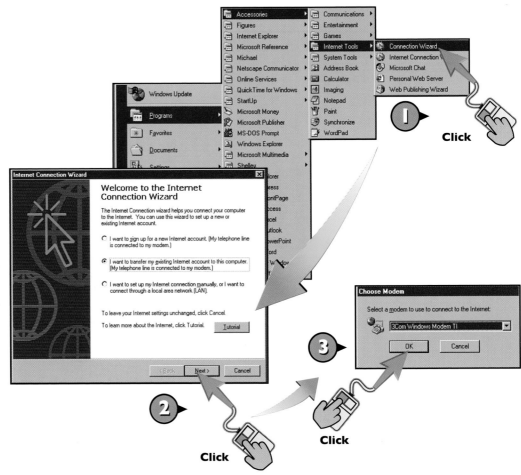

Click

Click

Click

✓ No Account?

If you do not have an ISP and you want Windows to find one for you, choose the first option in step 2 and then follow the wizard's directions.

✓ Manual Setup

This task shows you how to set up your Internet account manually—that is, if it does not appear in the list shown in step 4.

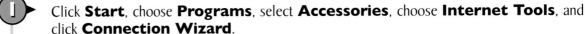

1 Click **Start**, choose **Programs**, select **Accessories**, choose **Internet Tools**, and click **Connection Wizard**.

2 If you have an Internet account, click the second radio button and click **Next**.

3 Select the modem to use and click **OK**.

Next Step

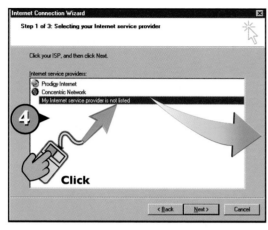

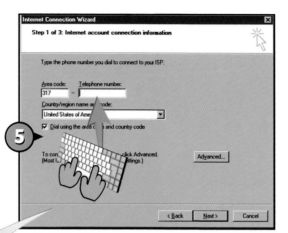

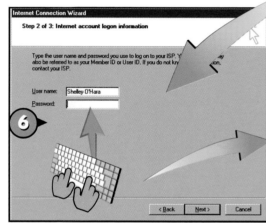

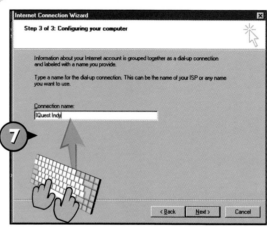

(4) If your ISP is listed, select it, click **Next**, and follow the instructions. If not, select **My Internet service provider is not listed** and click **Next** twice.

(5) Type the phone number for your ISP and click **Next**.

(6) Type your user name and the password assigned to you by your ISP. Then click **Next**.

(7) Type a name for your dial-up connection (you can use any name you want), and then click **Next**.

✓ **Finding an ISP**
You can find local ISPs in the Yellow Pages. There are also nationwide providers, such as AT&T WorldNet (you can get information about this provider from the Online Services folder), MindSpring, and EarthLink. Be sure to compare pricing and services when selecting an ISP.

Setting Up for the Internet Continued

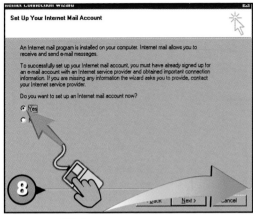

Click

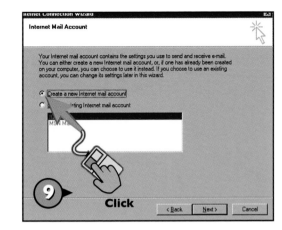

Click

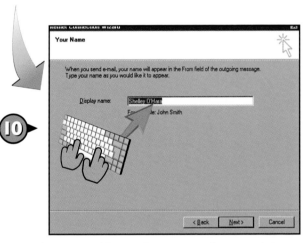

✓ **Go Back a Step**
If you need to change one
of your selections, click the
Back button to go back
through your choices.

 Select **Yes** if you want to set up your Internet mail account (this task assumes that you do), and then click **Next**.

Specify whether you want to use an existing mail account or to create a new account (this task assumes you want to set up a new account), and then click **Next**.

 Type the name you want displayed in messages, and then click **Next**.

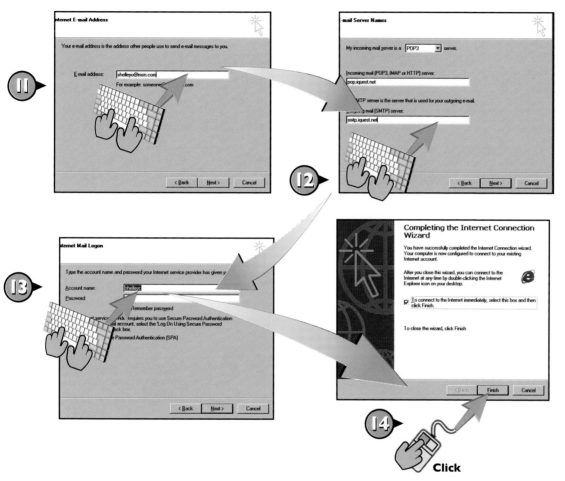

Click

 Type the email address assigned to you by your ISP, and then click **Next**.

 Enter the requested information about your incoming and outgoing mail servers (you can get this information from your ISP), and then click **Next**.

 Specify logon instructions, and then click **Next**.

 Click **Finish**.

 Cancel Setup
To cancel the setup, click the Cancel button.

Task 4: Starting Internet Explorer

Once you've got your Internet connection set up, you can start Internet Explorer and browse the Internet. To start, take a look at the different tools for browsing the Web.

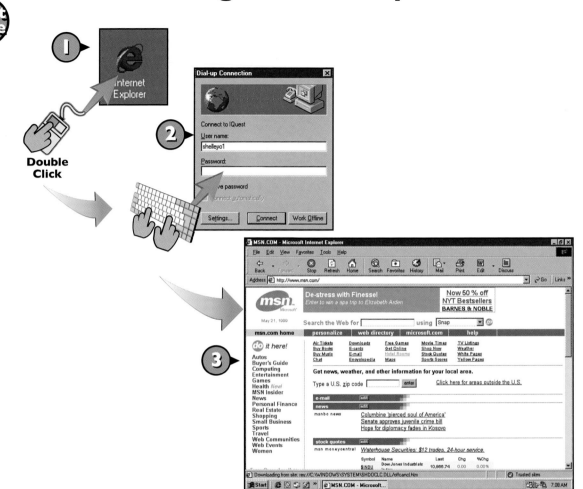

Start Here

Double Click

 Go Home
You can go to the start page (called your home page) at any time by clicking the **Home** button.

 Problems?
If you have problems connecting—the line is busy, for instance—try again. If you continue to have problems, check with your **ISP**.

1 Double-click the **Internet Explorer** icon.

2 Enter your user name and password (some information might have been completed for you), and then click the **Connect** button.

3 Windows connects to your ISP. The **Internet Explorer** window appears, and you see your start page, usually the MSN home page.

 End Task

Task 5: Typing an Address

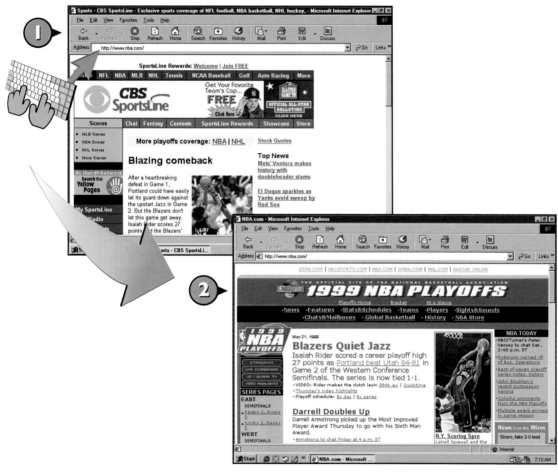

Typing a site's address is the fastest way to get to that site. An address, or *URL* (uniform resource locator), consists of the protocol (usually **http://**) and the domain name (something like **www.nba.com**). The domain name might also include a path (a list of folders) to the document. The extension (usually **.com, .net, .gov, .edu,** or **.mil**) indicates the type of site (commercial, network resources, government, educational, or military, respectively).

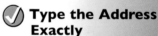 **Type the Address Exactly**
Make sure you type the address correctly. You must type the periods, colons, slashes, and other characters in the exact order.

Use AutoComplete
If you have typed an address before, you can type only its first few letters; Internet Explorer will display the rest.

1 ▸ In the **Address** bar, type the address of the site you want to visit, and then press **Enter**.

2 ▸ Internet Explorer displays the page associated with the URL you typed.

Information on the Internet is easy to browse because documents contain *links* to other pages, documents, and sites. Simply click a link to view the associated page. You can jump from link to link, exploring all types of topics and levels of information. Links are also called *hyperlinks*, and usually appear underlined and sometimes in a different color. You can also use the buttons in the toolbar to navigate from page to page.

✓ **Error Message**
If you see an error message when you click a link, it could indicate that the link is not accurate or that the server is too busy. Try again later.

✓ **Using Links Buttons**
Click any of the buttons in the **Links** toolbar to see some sites selected by Microsoft. You can select to view sites in several categories. The figures in this task show the links from the Sports page.

Task 6: Browsing with Links and Toolbar Buttons

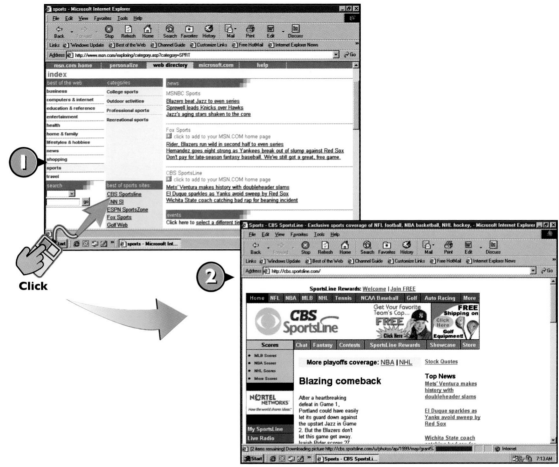

Click

1 ▶ From the MSN sports page, click a link (in this case, **CBS Sportsline**).

2 ▶ The page for that link appears (in this case, **www.cbs.sportsline.com**). Click the **Back** button in the toolbar to go to the last page you visited.

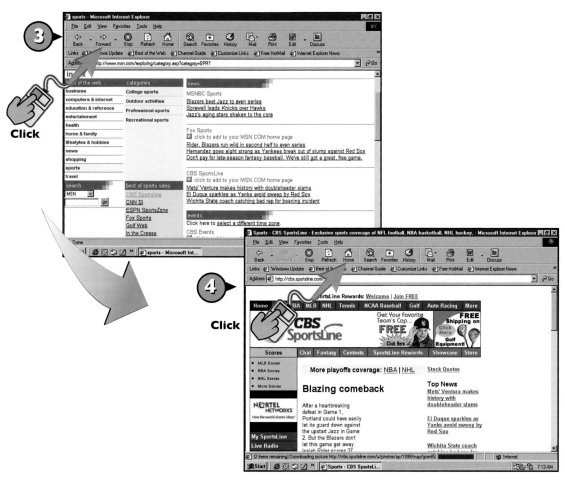

Click the **Forward** button to move forward through the pages you've already visited (you must have clicked the **Back** button before you can use the **Forward** button).

To return to the MSN start page, click the **Home** button in the toolbar.

Task 7: Adding a Site to Your Favorites List

Start Here

When you find a site that you especially like, you might want a quick way to return to it without having to browse from link to link or having to remember the address. Fortunately, Internet Explorer enables you to build a list of favorite sites and to access those sites by clicking them in the list.

✓ **Subscribe to a Site**
You can subscribe to sites and be alerted when the content has been updated. See the online help for information about subscribing to a site.

✓ **Download for Offline Review**
You can set up Internet Explorer to download the site so that you can review the information offline. Less time online can mean smaller ISP bills!

✓ **Removing a Site**
To remove a site from your Favorites list, choose Favorites, and then click Organize Favorites. Select the site you want to delete, and then click the Delete button. Confirm the deletion by clicking the Yes button.

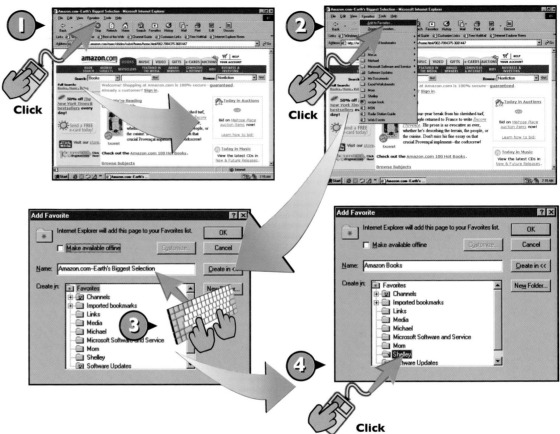

Click

Click

Click

After you've opened the Web site that you want to add to your **Favorites** list, click the **Favorites** option in the menu bar (do not click the **Favorites** button in the toolbar).

Click the **Add to Favorites** command.

Type a name for the page if you're not satisfied with the default name that is provided.

Select a folder for the link, and click **OK**.

End Task

Task 8: Going to a Site in Your Favorites List

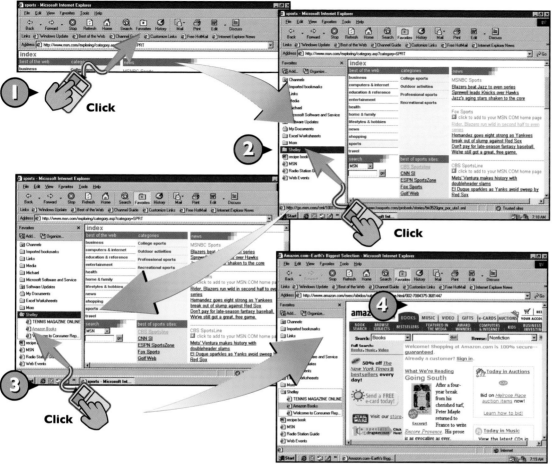

Click

Click

Click

After you have added a site to your **Favorites** list, you can easily reach that site by displaying the list and selecting the site.

✓ **Close Pane**
To close the **Favorites** pane, click its **Close** button.

✓ **Rearrange List**
You can also reach a site by opening the **Favorites** menu, and you can set up folders to group sites together. All of the sites and folders are listed. Simply select the folder you want (if necessary) and then select the site you want. For more information on adding folders, see the next task.

1 ▶ Click the **Favorites** button on the toolbar.

2 ▶ The pane on the left side of the screen contains your **Favorites** list, while the right-hand pane contains the current page. Click the folder you want to visit.

3 ▶ Click the site you want to visit.

4 ▶ Internet Explorer displays the site you selected from the **Favorites** list.

Task 9: Rearranging Your Favorites List

If you add several sites to your **Favorites** list, it might become difficult to use. You can organize the list by grouping similar sites together in a folder. You can add new folders and move sites from one folder to another.

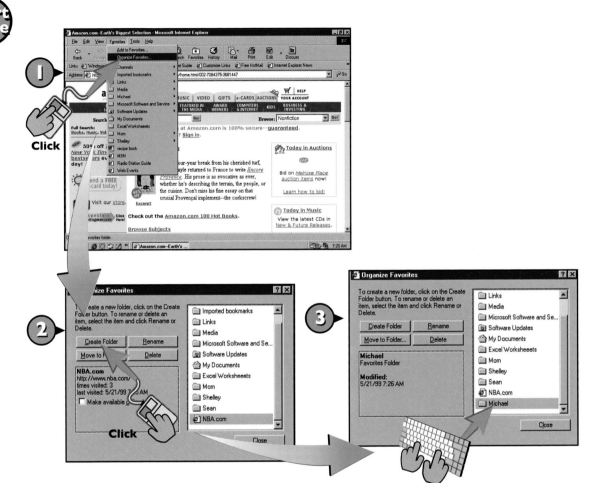

✓ **Dragging a Site**
You can drag a site from the list to the folder where you want to place the site.

1 ▶ Click the **Favorites** option in the menu bar and then choose **Organize Favorites**.

2 ▶ To create a new folder, click the **Create Folder** button.

3 ▶ Type the folder name and press **Enter**.

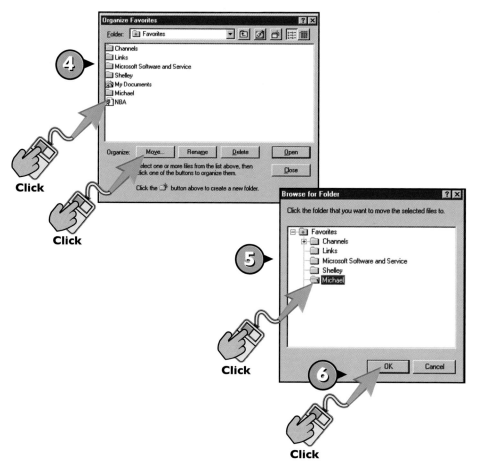

Click

Click

Click

Click

✅ **Deleting a Site**
To delete a site, select it and click the **Delete** button. Click the **Yes** button to confirm the deletion.

✅ **Renaming a Site**
To rename a site, select the site and click the **Rename** button. Type a new name, and press **Enter**.

④ ▶ To move a site from one folder to another, select the site, and then click the **Move to Folder** button.

⑤ ▶ Select the folder to which you want to move the site, and then click **OK**.

⑥ ▶ When you are finished moving all the sites you want to rearrange, click the **OK** button.

End Task

Task 10: Searching the Internet

The Internet includes *many* different sites. Looking for the site you want by browsing can be like looking for a needle in a haystack. Instead, you can search for a topic, and find all sites related to that topic. To search, you select to use either a search engine or a search index. The basic procedure is the same, but the results and special options for each search engine/index will vary.

✓ Move Search Options

You can refine a search and set search options. You can also find more information about the site, such as reviews or ratings, from some search tools. The search tool usually lists the "best" matches first. Look for a link at the end of the list to display the next set of matches.

✓ Topic Not Found?

If you don't find the topic you want, you can try a different search engine. The results may be different.

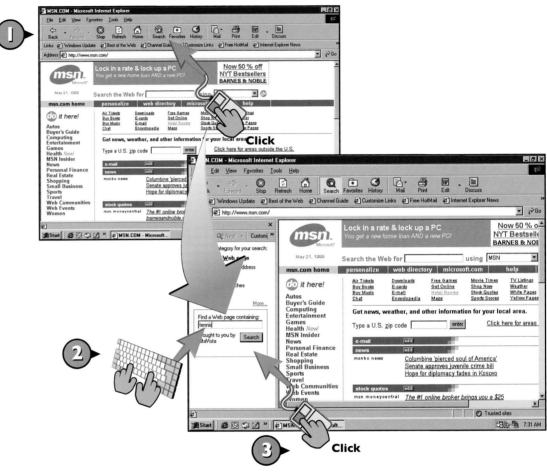

1 ▶ Click the **Search** button in the toolbar.

2 ▶ Type the word or phrase you want to find.

3 ▶ Click the **search** button. (The name of the button will vary depending on which provider you use.)

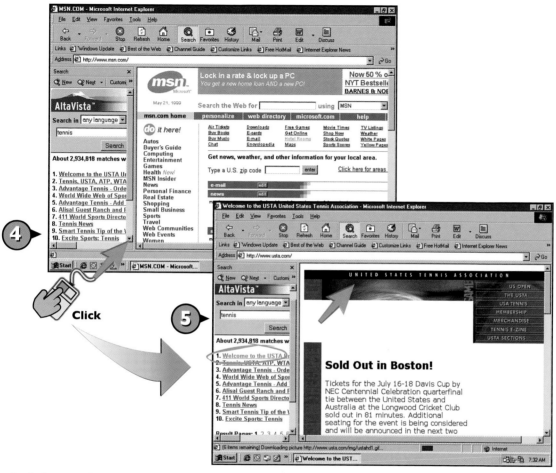

Click

4 The left pane displays the results of the search in link format. Scroll down until you find the link you want, and then click it.

5 The page you selected appears in the right-hand pane.

✓ **Scrolling Through the Results**
You can scroll through the Search bar to see all the results. To close the Search bar, click its **Close** button.

✓ **Use a Different Search Tool**
To select a different provider (search tool), display the **Choose provider** drop-down list and select the provider you want to use.

Task 11: Setting Internet Security Levels

With Internet Explorer 4, you can assign different zones to various sites, and assign a security level to each zone. Assign the **Local** zone to sites on your intranet; assign the **Trusted** zone to any sites from which it is safe to download and run files; assign the **Restricted** zone to sites from which it is not safe to download and run files. The **Internet** zone is assigned to all other sites by default. A site's assigned zone is displayed in the status bar.

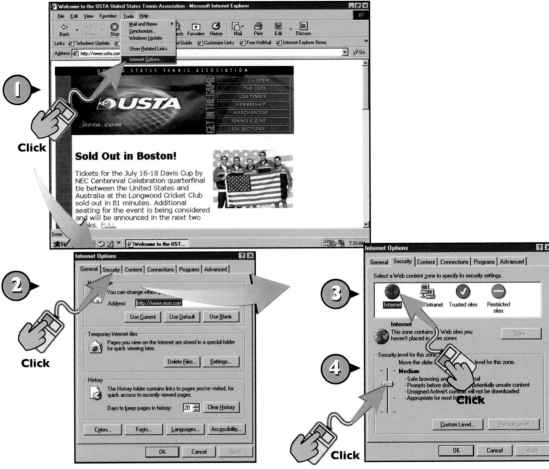

Click

Click

Click

Click

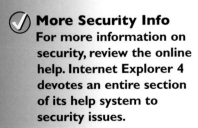

✓ More Security Info
For more information on security, review the online help. Internet Explorer 4 devotes an entire section of its help system to security issues.

1 ▶ To view information about zones or to alter the settings of a zone, click **Tools**, and then choose **Internet Options**.

2 ▶ Click the **Security** tab in the **Internet Options** dialog box.

3 ▶ To set the security level for a zone, select it in the **Zone** area.

4 ▶ Drag the slider bar to set the security level.

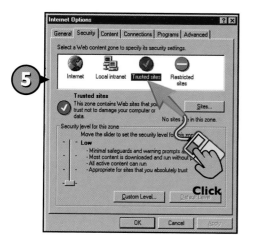

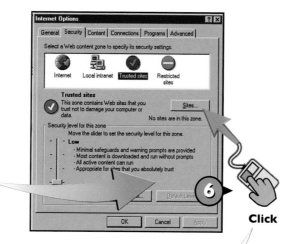

Click

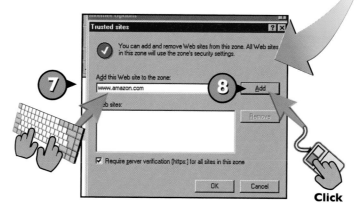

Click

✓ Removing Sites from a Zone
To remove a site from a zone, choose **View**, and then select **Internet Options.** Click the **Security** tab, display the zone assigned to the site you want to remove, and then click the **Add Sites** button. Select the site to be removed and click the **Remove** button. Click **OK** twice to exit the dialog boxes.

✓ Adding More Sites
Repeat steps 7 and 8 for each site you want to add to the zone.

5 To add Web sites to a particular zone, select the zone.

6 Click the **Sites** button.

7 Type the address of the site you want to add to the zone.

8 Click the **Add** button.

End Task

Task 12: Setting Your Home Page

Your home page is the first page you that see each time you log on to Internet Explorer. You can select the page you want as your home page.

Start Here

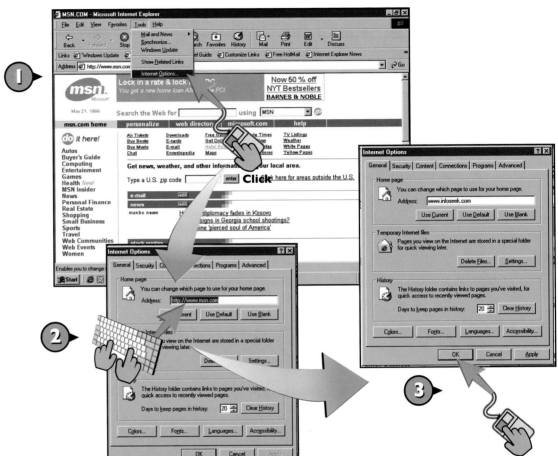

✓ **Use the Current Page**
To use the current page for the home page, click the **Use Current** button.

✓ **Go Back to the Default**
To go back to using the default home page, click the **Use Default** button.

1 ▶ Click **Tools** and choose **Internet Options**.

2 ▶ Type the address of the page you want for your home page.

3 ▶ Click **OK**. Now when you click the **Home** button, this is the page Internet Explorer will display.

End Task

Task 13: Using the History List

As you browse from link to link, you might remember a site that you liked, but not remember that site's name or address. You can easily return to sites you have visited by displaying the **History** list. From this list, you can select the week you want to review, and then the site you want to visit.

✅ **Closing the List**
To close the **History** list, click the **Close** button in the top-right corner of the **History** bar.

✅ **How Long Kept**
You can select how many days the history is kept, and you can clear the **History** list. Choose **View**, click **Internet Options**, and then select the number of days the history should be kept. To clear the history, click the **Clear History** button.

1 ▸ Click the **History** button.

2 ▸ Internet Explorer displays the **History** list in a pane on the left side of the window. If necessary, select the week whose list you want to review.

3 ▸ Click the site you want. Internet Explorer displays that site.

Task 14: Starting Outlook Express

You can use **Outlook Express** to create, send, and receive email over the Internet. You can also send files by attaching them to your messages.

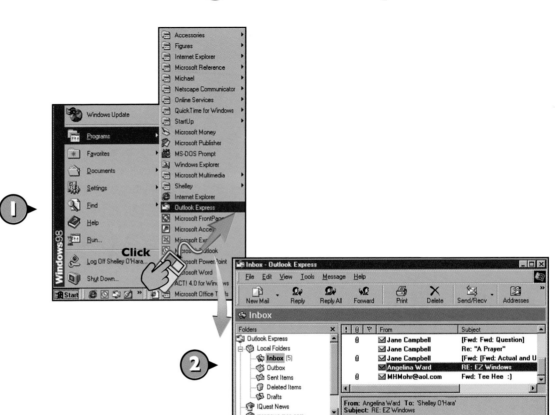

✓ Set Up First
To use Outlook, your computer must be configured for use over the Internet.

✓ Close Outlook Express
To close Outlook Express, choose **File** and then click **Close.** If Windows prompts you to disconnect from the network, choose **Yes.**

✓ Start From Toolbar
To start Outlook Express from Internet Explorer 4, click the **Mail** button and choose **Read Mail.** To start Outlook Express from the Quick Launch toolbar, click the **Launch Outlook Express** button.

 Click **Start,** choose the **Programs** command, and then click **Outlook Express**.

 Outlook Express is started.

Task 15: Reading Mail

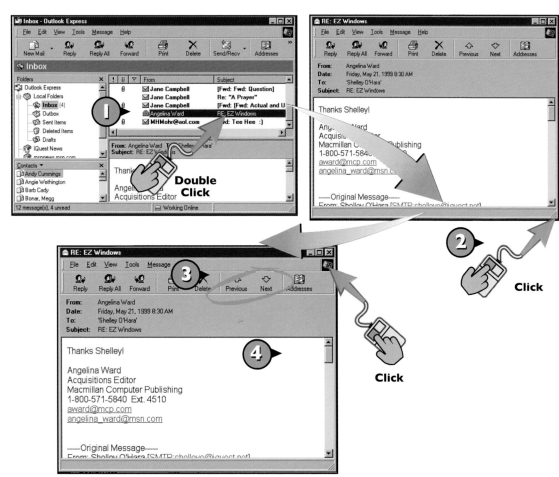

Double Click

Click

Click

When you start Outlook Express and get connected to your ISP, the messages are downloaded from your Internet mail server to your computer. The number of messages in your inbox appears in parentheses next to the inbox link in the folder list (the pane on the left-hand side of the screen). The message list (the upper-right pane) lists all messages. Messages appearing in bold have not yet been read, but you can open and read any message in the message list.

 Print Message
To print an open message, choose **File**, select **Print**, and then click **OK** in the **Print** dialog box. To save an open message, choose **File** and then click **Save As**. Assign the message a filename and location, and then click **Save**.

 Delete Message
To delete a message, choose **File** and then click **Delete**, or click the **Delete** button in the toolbar.

 In the message list of the **Outlook Express** window, double-click the message you want to read.

 The message you selected is displayed in its own window. You can scroll through the contents to read the message.

 To display the next message in the message list, click the up arrow; to display the previous message in the message list, click the down arrow.

 To close the message, click the **Close** button.

Task 16: Setting Email Preferences

You have lots of options on how messages are sent and delivered. To review and make changes to these options, use the **Options** dialog box from Outlook Express.

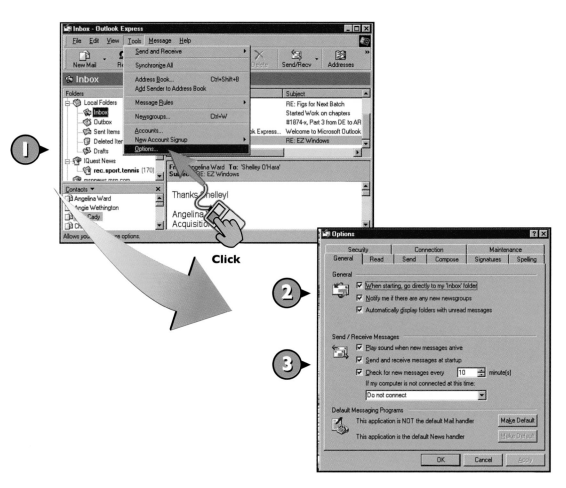

Click

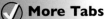

More Tabs

The most common options are included on the General tab, but you can also display other tabs to review and change other options, including the Read, Send, Compose, and Security tabs.

 Click **Tools** and select **Options**.

 On the **General** tab, adjust the options in the **General** area to best suit your needs.

 Adjust the settings in the **Send/Receive Messages** area, and click **OK**.

End Task

Task 17: Responding to Mail

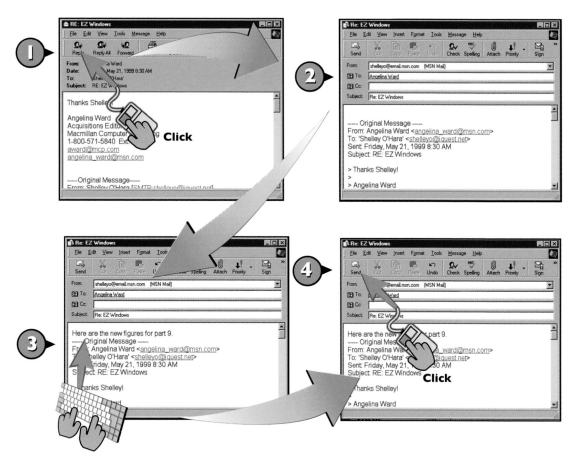

You can easily respond to a message you've received. Outlook Express completes the address and subject lines for you; you can then simply type the response.

① Display the message to which you want to reply, and click the **Reply** button in the toolbar.

② The address and subject lines are completed, and the text of the original message is appended to the bottom of the reply message.

③ Type your message.

④ Click the **Send** button.

✓ **Forward Message**
To forward a message, click the **Forward** command in the **Compose** menu or click the **Forward** button. Type the address of the recipient, and then click in the message area and type any message you want to include. Then click the **Send** button.

✓ **Using Menu**
You can also click the **Reply to Author** command in the **Compose** menu.

Task 18: Creating and Sending Mail

You can send a message to anyone with an Internet email address. Simply type the recipient's email address, a subject, and the message. You can also send carbon copies (Cc) and blind carbon copies (Bcc) of messages, as well as attach files to your messages.

✓ **Use Toolbar**
You can also click the **New Mail** button in the toolbar to create a new message.

✓ **Address Is Wrong**
If you enter an incorrect address and the message is not sent, you most likely will receive a **Failure to Deliver** notice. Be sure to type the address in its proper format.

✓ **Attaching a File**
To attach a file—such as a spreadsheet or word-processing document—to your message, choose **Insert** and then click **File Attachment,** or click the **Insert File** button. In the **Insert Attachment** dialog box, choose the file you want to attach and click the **Attach** button.

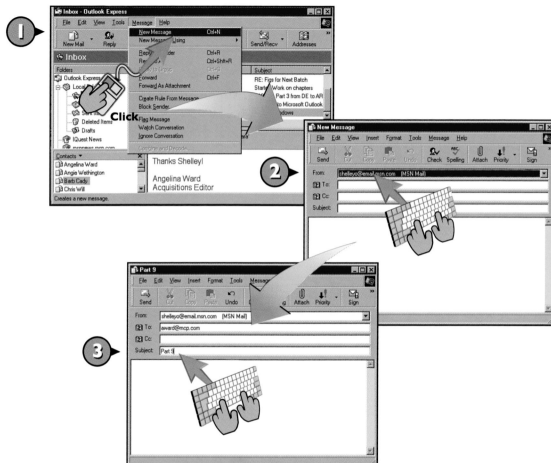

1 In the **Outlook Express** window, click **Message** and then choose **New Message**.

2 Type the recipient's address (as well any necessary Cc and Bcc addresses). Addresses are in the format **username@domainname.ext** (for example, **award@mcp.com**). Press **Tab**.

3 Type a subject in the **Subject** text box, and then press **Tab**.

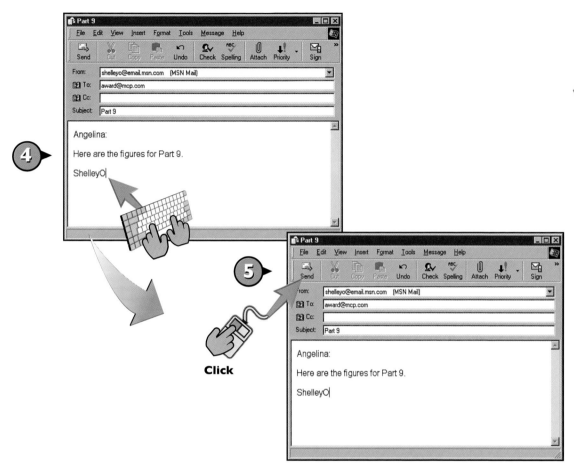

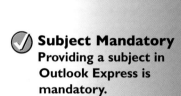

Click

4 ▸ Type your message.

5 ▸ When you've completed the message, click the **Send** button.

✓ **Subject Mandatory**
Providing a subject in Outlook Express is mandatory.

✓ **What Happens with Send**
If you are connected to the Internet, the message is sent when the **Send** button is clicked. If you're not connected to the Internet, Windows places the message in the **Outbox**, where it remains until the next time you connect to your ISP. You can connect and send the message by clicking the **Send and Receive** button.

Task 19: Looking Up an Email Address

The Internet includes several directories for finding people (email addresses and other information). You can look up this information from Outlook Express.

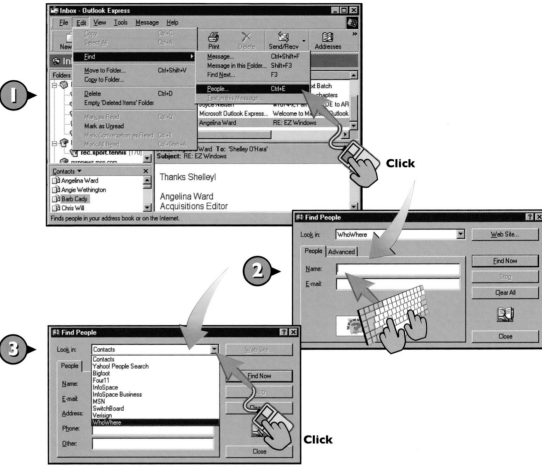

Click

Click

1. Open the **Edit** menu, choose **Find**, and select **People**.

2. Display the **Look in** drop-down list and select the directory you want to use.

3. Type the person's name.

Next Step

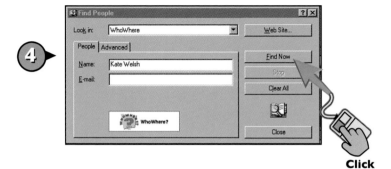

Click

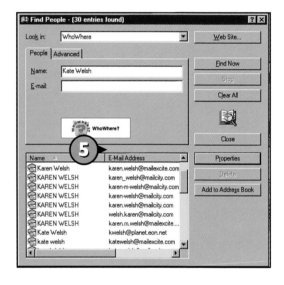

 Click the **Find Now** button.

 You see the results of the search.

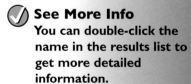 **See More Info**
You can double-click the name in the results list to get more detailed information.

Task 20: Subscribing to Newsgroups

Start Here

A *newsgroup* is a collection of messages relating to a particular topic. Anyone can post a message, and anyone who subscribes to the newsgroup can view and respond to posted messages. You can join any of hundreds of thousands of newsgroups on the Internet to exchange information and learn about hobbies, businesses, pets, computers, people of different walks of life, and more. You use Outlook Express for both email and newsgroups.

 Viewing the First Time
The first time you select your newsgroup, you see a dialog box asking whether you want to view a list of the available newsgroups. Follow the onscreen instructions for viewing and subscribing to a newsgroup.

 Search the Newsgroups List
You can search for a specific word—for example, **computers** or **banjo**—by entering the word in the **Display Newsgroups Which Contain** text box.

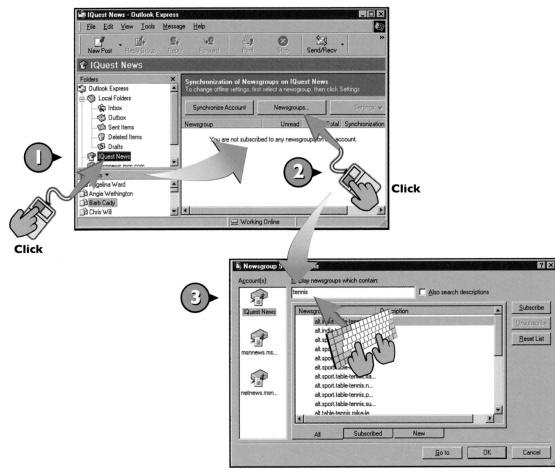

Click

Click

1 ▶ In the **Outlook Express** folder list, click your news server.

2 ▶ Click the **Newsgroups** button in order to subscribe to a newsgroup.

3 ▶ In the **Display newsgroups which contain** text box, type the name of a topic area that interests you (I've typed **tennis**).

Next Step

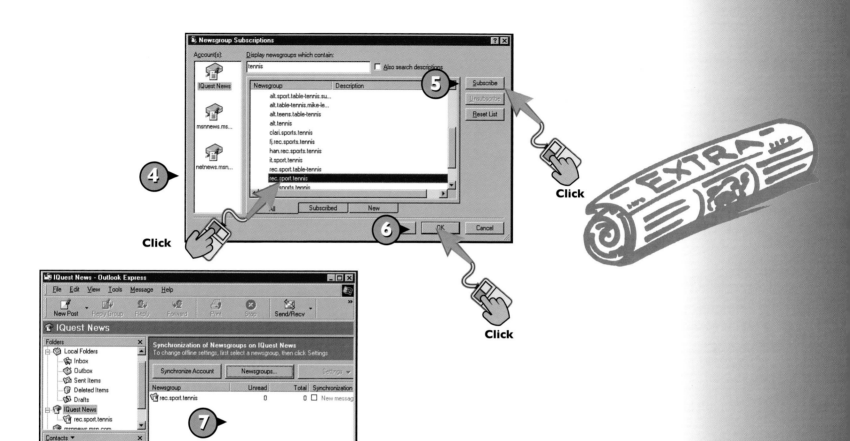

Click

Click

Click

4 Select a newsgroup from the **Newsgroups** list.

5 Click the **Subscribe** button.

6 Click **OK**.

7 The newsgroup is added to your news server list.

✓ **Unsubscribe**
To unsubscribe to a newsgroup, click the **Newsgroups** button. Select the newsgroup to which you want to unsubscribe and then click the **Unsubscribe** button.

End Task

Task 21: Reading Newsgroup Messages

After you have subscribed to a newsgroup, you can review any of the messages in that group. When a new message is posted, it starts a *thread*, and all responses are part of this thread. You can review all the current messages in the thread.

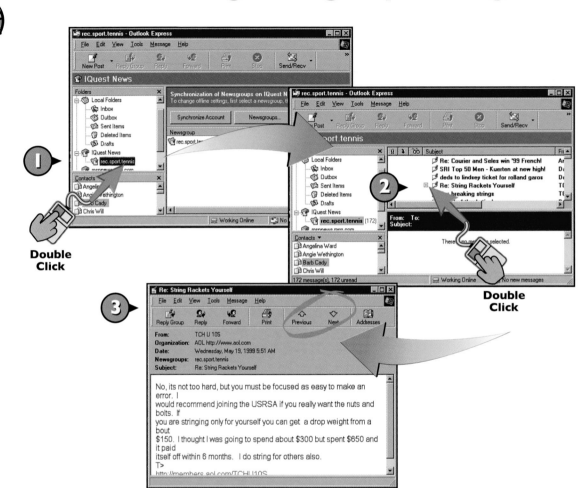

Double
Click

Double
Click

✅ **Don't Like the Newsgroup?**
Keep in mind that newsgroups are not usually monitored. You might come across messages that you find offensive. If so, it's best to just unsubscribe from that newsgroup.

✅ **Print Message**
To print a message, select it in the window, click **File** and choose **Print**. To save a message, select it, click **File**, and then choose **Save Message**. Then assign the message a location on your hard drive and click **OK**.

1 In the folder list of the **Outlook Express** window, double-click the newsgroup you want to review.

2 A list of that newsgroup's messages appears in the message list. Messages in bold have not yet been read; messages with a plus sign have responses. Double-click the message you want to read.

3 The message opens. To display the next message, click the up arrow; to display the previous message, click the down arrow. To close the message, click the **Close** button.

Next
Step

Task 22: Replying to an Existing Newsgroup Message

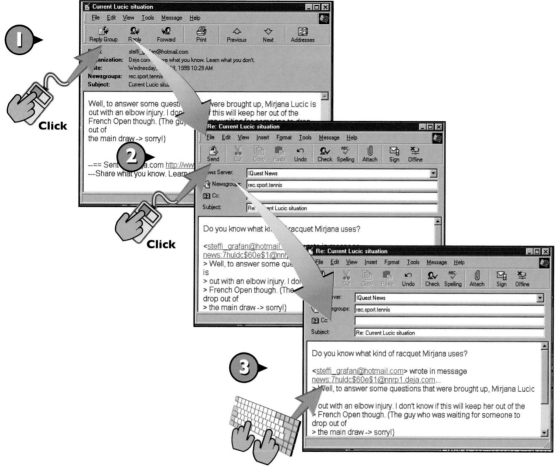

Click

Click

If you come across a newsgroup message to which you want to respond, you can post a reply to that message.

 Display the message to which you want to reply. Click the **Reply Group** button.

 Type your message.

 Click the **Send** button.

 Replying via Email
You can also reply to messages privately by emailing the author. To send an email message, click the **Reply** button. Type your message, and click the **Send** button.

Task 23: Posting New Messages

After you review messages, you might want to post your own opinion. One way to do this is to post a new message, or start a new thread.

Start Here

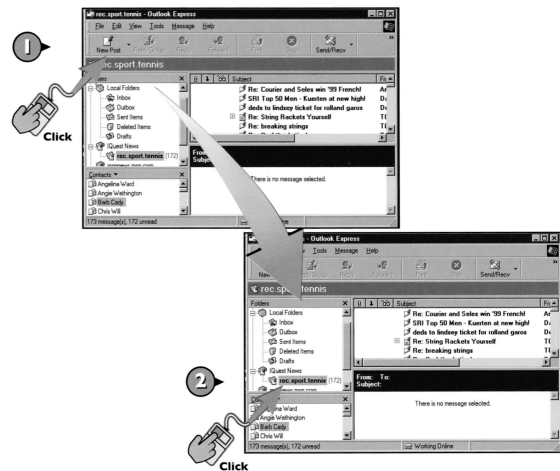

Click

Click

✓ **Canceling a Message**
If you change your mind about posting a message, you can cancel the message if you have not already clicked **Send**. Simply click the message's **Close** button and, when prompted, click the **Yes** button to confirm that you don't want to save the message.

1 ▶ In the folders list, select the newsgroup to which you want to post a new message.

2 ▶ Click the **New Post** button.

Next
Step ▶

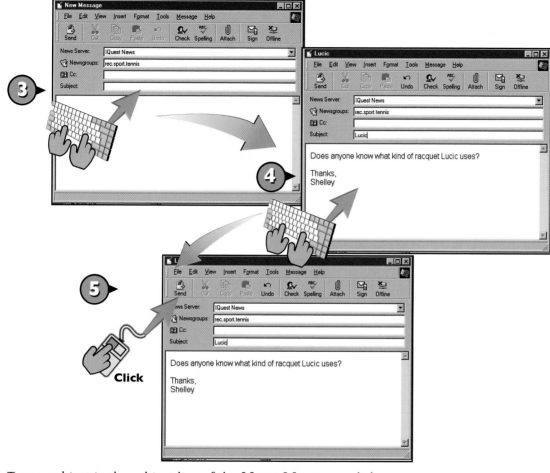

3▶ Type a subject in the subject line of the **New Message** dialog.

4▶ Type your message.

5▶ Click the **Post** button on the toolbar.

A

accessory   One of the miniapplications that comes free with Windows 98. Examples include WordPad, Paint, and Backup.

Active Desktop   The new Windows 98 *desktop*, which lets you replace the static desktop of Windows 95 with one that can hold Web pages and miniprograms (such as a clock, a stock ticker, or a weather map).

active window   The window you're currently using. You can tell a window is active by looking at its title bar: If the bar shows white letters on a dark back-ground, the window is active. Inactive windows show light gray letters on a dark gray background.

application   Software that accomplishes a specific practical task. It's basically the same thing as a *program*.

application window   A window that contains a running application, such as Explorer or WordPad.

ASCII text file   A file that uses only the American Standard Code for Information Interchange character set (techno-lingo for the characters you see on your keyboard).

B

backup job   A Microsoft Backup file that includes a list of files to back up, the type of backup to use (*full*, *differential*, or *incremental*), and the backup destination.

boot   To start your computer. The term *booting* comes from the phrase "pulling oneself up by one's own bootstraps," which refers to the fact that your computer can load everything it needs to operate properly without any help from you.

bps   Bits per second. The rate at which a *modem* or other communications device spits data through a phone line or cable.

browser   A program that you use to *surf* sites on the World Wide Web. The browser that comes with Windows 98 is called Internet Explorer.

byte   A single character of information.

C

cascade menu   A menu that appears when you select certain pull-down menu commands.

CD-ROM drive   A special computer disk drive that's designed to handle CD-ROM discs, which resemble audio CDs. CD-ROMs have enormous capacity (about 500 times that of a typical *floppy disk*), so they're most often used to hold large applications, graphics libraries, and huge collections of junky shareware programs.

channel   A special World Wide Web site that features changing content that is sent automatically to your computer at predefined intervals. See *subscription*.

character formatting   Changing the look of text characters by altering their font, size, style, and more.

character spacing   The amount of space a font reserves for each character. In a *monospaced font*, every character gets the same amount of space regardless of its true width. In a *proportional font*, the space allotted to each letter varies according to the width of the letter.

check box   A square-shaped switch that toggles a dialog box option on or off. The option is toggled on when a check mark appears in the box.

classic view   The folder view used with Windows 95. That is, you click an icon to select it, and you double-click an icon to launch it. See also *Web view*.

click   To quickly press and release the left mouse button.

Clipboard   An area of memory that holds data temporarily during cut and paste operations.

command button   A rectangular "button" (usually found in dialog boxes) that, when clicked, runs whatever command is spelled out on it.

commands   The options you see in a pull-down menu. You use these commands to tell the application what you want it to do next.

D

data files   The files used by you or your programs. See also *program files*.

delay   The amount of time it takes for a second character to appear when you press and hold down a key.

desktop   A metaphor for the Windows 98 screen. Starting a Windows 98 application is similar to putting a folder full of papers (the application window) on your desk. To do some work, you pull some papers out of the folder (the document windows) and place them on the desktop.

device driver   A small program that controls the way a device (such as a mouse) works with your system.

dialog boxes   Windows that pop up on the screen to ask you for information or to seek confirmation of an action you requested.

differential backup   Backs up only files in the current *backup job* that have changed since the last *full backup*. See also *incremental backup*.

digital camera   A special camera that saves pictures, using digital storage (such as a memory card) instead of film.

directory

directory   See *folder*.

diskette   See *floppy disk*.

docking station   A component that a notebook computer can attach to. The docking station provides ports for plugging in a regular monitor, keyboard, and mouse, as well as a number of expansion bays and other items that are usually too bulky to work with the notebook by itself.

document window   A window opened in an application. Document windows hold whatever you're working on in the application.

double-click   To quickly press and release the left mouse button *twice* in succession.

double-click speed   The maximum amount of time Windows 98 allows between the mouse clicks of a double-click.

drag   To press and hold down the left mouse button and then move the mouse.

drag-and-drop   A technique you use to run commands or move things around; you use your mouse to *drag* files or icons to strategic screen areas and drop them there.

drop-down list box   A list box that normally shows only a single item but, when selected, displays a list of options.

F

file   An organized unit of information inside your computer.

floppy disk   A portable storage medium that consists of a flexible disk protected by a plastic case. Floppy disks are available in a variety of sizes and capacities.

focus   The window that has the attention of the operating system (that is, Windows 98). See also *active window*.

folder   A storage location on your hard disk in which you keep related files together.

font   A character set of a specific typeface, type style, and type size.

format bar   A series of text boxes and buttons that enable you to format the characters in your document. The format bar typically appears under the toolbar.

formatting   The process of setting up a disk so that a drive can read its information and write information to it. Not to be confused with *character formatting*.

fragmented   When a single file is chopped up and stored in separate chunks scattered around a hard disk. You can fix this by running Windows 98's Disk Defragmenter program.

fritterware   Any software that causes you to fritter away time fiddling with its various bells and whistles.

full backup   Backs up all the files in the current *backup job*. See also *differential backup* and *incremental backup*.

G-H-I

gigabyte   1,024 *megabytes*. Those in-the-know usually abbreviate this as **GB** when writing, and as **gig** when speaking. See also *byte*, *kilobyte*, and *megabyte*.

hard disk   The main storage area inside your computer.

hover   To place the mouse pointer over an object for a few seconds. In most Windows applications, for example, if you hover the mouse over a toolbar button, a small banner shows up that tells you the name of the button.

icons   The little pictures that Windows 98 uses to represent programs and files.

incremental backup   Backs up only files in the current *backup job* that have changed since the last *full backup* or the last *differential backup*.

infrared port   A communications port, usually found on notebook computers and some printers. Infrared ports enable two devices to communicate by using infrared light waves instead of cables.

insertion point cursor   The blinking vertical bar you see inside a text box or in a word-processing application, such as WordPad. It indicates where the next character you type will appear.**Internet**   A *network* of networks that extends around the world. By setting up an account with an Internet service provider, you can access this network.

intranet   The implementation of *Internet* technologies for use within a corporate organization rather than for connection to the Internet as a whole.

IR   Short for infrared. See *infrared port*.

J-K-L

Jaz drive   A special disk drive that uses portable disks (about the size of *floppy disks*) that hold 1 *gigabyte* of data.

Kbps

Kbps   One thousand bits per second (*bps*). Today's modern *modems* transmit data at either 28.8Kbps or 56Kbps.

kilobyte   1,024 *bytes*. This is often abbreviated to **K** or **KB**. See also *megabyte* and *gigabyte*.

LAN   See *local area network*.

local area network   A *network* in which all the computers occupy a relatively small geographical area, such as a department, an office, a home, or a building. All the connections between computers are made via network cables.

list box   A small window that displays a list of items such as filenames or directories.

M

maximize   To increase the size of a window to its largest extent. A maximized application window fills the entire screen (except for the taskbar). A maximized document window fills the entire application window.

Mbps   One million bits per second (*bps*).

megabyte   1,024 *kilobytes* or 1,048,576 *bytes*. This is often abbreviated in writing to **M** or **MB** and pronounced **meg**. See also *gigabyte*.

memory-resident program   A program that stays in memory after it is loaded and works "behind the scenes." The program normally responds only to a specific event (such as the deletion of a file) or key combination. Also called a *terminate-and-stay-resident* (TSR) program.

menu bar   The horizontal bar on the second line of an application window. The menu bar contains the application's pull-down menus.

minimize   To remove a program from the desktop without closing it. A button for the program remains on the taskbar.

modem   An electronic device that enables two computers to exchange data over phone lines.

multitasking   The capability to run several programs at the same time.

N-O-P

network   A collection of computers connected via special cables or other network media (such as *infrared ports*) to share files, folders, disks, peripherals, and applications. See also *local area network*.

newsgroup   An Internet discussion group devoted to a single topic. These discussions progress by "posting" messages to the group.

option buttons   See *radio buttons*.

point   To place the mouse pointer so that it rests on a specific screen location.

port   The connection into which you plug the cable from a device such as a mouse or printer.

program files   The files that run your programs. See also *data files*.

pull-down menus   Hidden menus that you open from an application's menu bar to access the commands and features of the application.

R

radio buttons   Dialog box options that appear as small circles in groups of two or more. Only one option from a group can be chosen. These are also called *option buttons*.

RAM   Stands for random access memory. The memory in your

computer that Windows 98 uses to run your programs.

repeat rate   After the initial delay, the rate at which characters appear when you press and hold down a key.

right-click   To click the right mouse button instead of the usual left button. In Windows 98, right-clicking something usually pops up a *shortcut menu*.

S

scalable font   A font in which each character exists as an outline that can be scaled to different sizes. Windows 98 includes such scalable fonts as Arial, Courier New, and Times New Roman. To use scalable fonts, you must have a software program called a *type manager* to do the scaling. Windows 98 comes with its own type manager: TrueType.

scrollbar   A bar that appears at the bottom or on the right side of a window when the window is too small to display all its contents.

shortcut   A special file that points to a program or a document. Double-clicking the shortcut starts the program or loads the document.

shortcut menu   A menu that contains a few commands related to an item (such as the *desktop* or the *taskbar*). You display the shortcut menu by *right-clicking* the object.

subscription   A method of checking for new or changed data on a World Wide Web site or *channel*. The subscription sets up a schedule for checking a particular site to see whether it has changed in any way since the last time it was checked.

surf   To travel from site to site on the World Wide Web.

system menu   A menu, common to every Windows 98 window, that you use to manipulate various features of the window. You activate the **Control** menu by clicking the **Control Menu** box in the upper-left corner of the window or by pressing **Alt + spacebar** (for an application window).

system resources   Two memory areas that Windows 98 uses to keep track of things such as the position and size of open windows, dialog boxes, and your desktop configuration (wallpaper and so on).

T

taskbar   The horizontal strip across the bottom of the Windows 98 screen. Each running application is given its own taskbar button, and you switch to an application by clicking its button.

text box   A screen area in which you type text information, such as a description or a filename.

text editor   A program that lets you edit files that contain only text. The Windows 98 text editor is called Notepad.

title bar   The area on the top line of a window that displays the window's title.

toolbar   A series of application-specific buttons that typically appears beneath the menu bar.

tracking speed   The speed at which the mouse pointer moves across the screen when you move the mouse on its pad.

TrueType   A *font-management program* that comes with Windows 98.

type size   A measure of the height of a font. Type size is measured in *points*; there are 72 points in an inch.

type style   Character attributes, such as regular, bold, and italic. Other type styles (often called type *effects*) are underline and strikethrough.

typeface   A distinctive graphic design of letters, numbers, and other symbols.

W

Web integration   The integration of World Wide Web techniques into the Windows 98 interface. See *Web view*.

Web view   The folder view used when *Web integration* is activated. With this view, you *hover* the mouse over an icon to select it, and you click an icon to launch it. See also *classic view*.

window   A rectangular screen area in which Windows 98 displays applications and documents.

Page
262

word wrap   A word-processor feature that automatically starts a new line when your typing reaches the end of the current line.

write-protection   Floppy disk safeguard that prevents you from changing any information on the disk. The 5¼-inch disks normally have a small notch on the side of the disk. If the notch is covered with tape, the disk is write-protected. Simply remove the tape to disable the write-protection. On a 3½-inch disk, write-protection is controlled by a small movable tab on the back of the disk. If the tab is toward the edge of the disk, the disk is write-protected. To disable the write-protection, slide the tab away from the edge of the disk.

X-Y-Z

Zip drive   A special disk drive that uses portable disks (a little smaller than a *Jaz drive* disk), which hold 100 *megabytes* of data.

A

B

C

desktop

insertion points